Collins

Perfect
Maths
1

Prabha Sethy

Components of DigiSuite

Main menu · **Learning objects** · **Search book or online** · **Page jump** · **Mark-up data**

View fullscreen
Help menu
Bookmark page
Open tool panel
Insert note
Pen & highlight
Single/double page
Zoom in
Zoom out
Zoom 100%
Sound on/off
Record audio
Spotlight
Clear data

Interactive whiteboard mode — IWB

Collins DIGISUITE
Search here — Online Search

- All Pages
- Table of Contents
- Animation
- Audio
- Interactivities
- Teacher's Resource
- Learning Tools
- Test Generator
- Dictionary

Page 14-15 / 24

3 Addition up to 20

LEARNING OBJECTIVES
- To add numbers up to 20 and study addition facts
- To learn addition using number line
- To learn different number combinations
- To add two 1-digit numbers, and add 1-digit and 2-digit numbers
- To learn how to add three numbers
- To solve word problems on addition

LET'S GET STARTED

Asif and Ravi are celebrating the Earth day. They are cleaning the park by collecting the garbage. Radha, Anna and Riya also join them. These three girls start watering the saplings. So, there are two boys and three girls in the park now. How many children are there in all? Would you like to join them too? Why should we water the plants?

ADDING TWO NUMBERS

Riya and Soham went to the beach with their parents. While walking alongside the beach, Riya collected 4 seashells. Soham collected 3 seashells. Let us find out the total number of seashells that they have collected.

Seashells collected by Riya   Seashells collected by Soham

We know that 4 is greater than 3. To know the total number of seashells, we can count forward from the greater number which is 4.

3 more than 4

$$4 \quad 5 \quad 6 \quad 7$$

$$4 + 3 = 7$$

This is read as four plus three is equal to seven.

So, Riya and Soham collected 7 seashells.

We can change the order of numbers in addition.

For example, the total number of frogs can be calculated as:

$$3 + 2 = 5 \quad \text{or} \quad 2 + 3 = 5$$

Therefore, when we count all the frogs, we see that there are 5 frogs in all.

The result of addition remains the same when numbers are added in any order.

Teacher-only

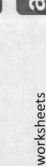

tn teacher's notes
ak answer keys
lp lesson plans
w worksheets
g games
v videos

Student + Teacher

ia activities
w worksheets
audio
a animations
ilt instructor-led tutorials

Preface

Perfect Maths is a series of eleven books for Classes Nursery to 8. The books for the Foundational Stage, previously referred to as Grades Nursery, Lower KG and Upper KG, would be the base to make the series complete in providing a strong foundation in numeracy, starting from ECCE till the middle stage. The series adheres to the guidelines of the **National Education Policy (NEP) 2020**, aligns with the vision of the *National Initiative for Proficiency in Reading with Understanding and Numeracy (NIPUN Bharat)* and aims to make mathematics more relevant to students in a non-threatening way.

The books for Foundational Stage 1 to 3 (Grades Nursery to UKG) are focused on the holistic development of a child. Based on **Numeracy Skills**, **21st Century Skills** and **Multiple Intelligences**, integrated and interdisciplinary approach, experiential learning, the books aim to help a child be "**Happy to Learn**". The unique blend of direct instructions, play-based structured activities, investigations, stories and rhymes provide the children ample opportunities to develop their numeracy and literacy skills.

The books for Classes 1 to 8 follow the *5E Learning Model*. The 5E Learning Model provides an activity-oriented approach to the series to make mathematics engaging for students through emphasizing connections between mathematics and day-to-day experiences. This series adheres to the guidelines of NEP 2020 completely, with the effective integration of its features with **21st Century Skills**, **Art Integration**, **Experiential Learning**, **Cross-curricular** and **India Focus**. The skill building questions and the varied exposure to situations provided in the pages of this series keep the learners at the centre and focus on making them future-ready. The series also aims to make students aware of the United Nations **Sustainable Development Goals** (SDGs), so that they can become SDG Pioneers, Champions or Ambassadors.

SAFAL in *Perfect Maths*: This series also strives to make a shift from rote-learning to competency-based learning, in accordance with **Structured Assessment For Analyzing Learning (SAFAL)**. The components of SAFAL—critical thinking, inquiry-based learning and analysis-based learning—are woven into the features such as Exercises, Mental Maths, Chapter Revision, Skill Up!, Worksheets, Reasoning Worksheets, Review/Assessment Corner and PISA Corner (Classes 6 to 8).

We would like to take this opportunity to thank all the teachers and educationist who reviewed the books and provided their feedback, which helped in improving the quality of the content.

Feedback, invaluable comments and suggestions from users are welcome.

Authors

About the Author

Prabha Sethy, formerly a teacher at Welham Boys' School, Dehradun, with more than 30 years of experience in teaching mathematics, brings in resources from everyday life into her content.

Key Features

The key features of *Perfect Maths* are completely aligned with the **National Education Policy (NEP) 2020** and the vision of the ***National Initiative for Proficiency in Reading with Understanding and Numeracy* (NIPUN Bharat)**. These meticulously designed features, based on the *5E Learning Model*, can be used as learning strategies to enhance the understanding of key concepts in mathematics and increase practical learning and problem-solving by bringing in real-life contexts from outside the classroom while providing some form of experiential learning. These key features also aim to help the learners shift from rote-learning to competency-based learning, in accordance with *Structured Assessment For Analyzing Learning* (SAFAL).

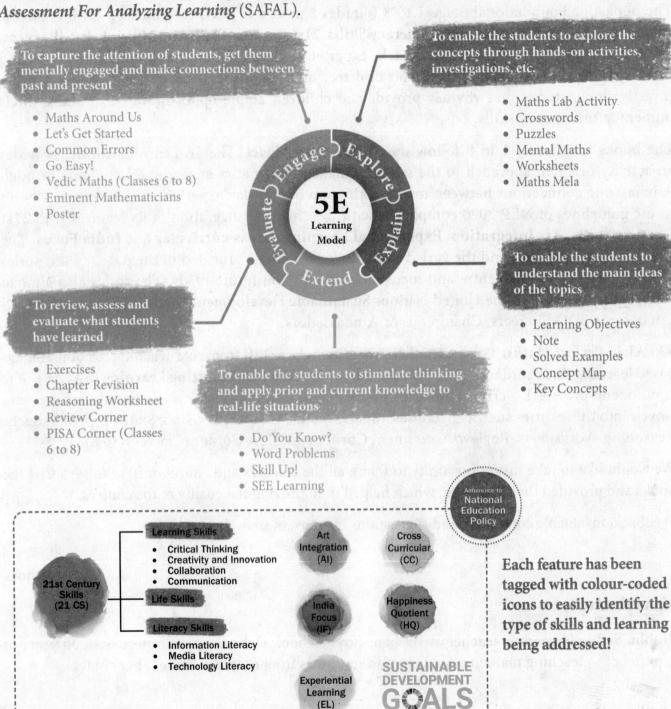

To capture the attention of students, get them mentally engaged and make connections between past and present

- Maths Around Us
- Let's Get Started
- Common Errors
- Go Easy!
- Vedic Maths (Classes 6 to 8)
- Eminent Mathematicians
- Poster

To enable the students to explore the concepts through hands-on activities, investigations, etc.

- Maths Lab Activity
- Crosswords
- Puzzles
- Mental Maths
- Worksheets
- Maths Mela

To enable the students to understand the main ideas of the topics

- Learning Objectives
- Note
- Solved Examples
- Concept Map
- Key Concepts

To review, assess and evaluate what students have learned

- Exercises
- Chapter Revision
- Reasoning Worksheet
- Review Corner
- PISA Corner (Classes 6 to 8)

To enable the students to stimulate thinking and apply prior and current knowledge to real-life situations

- Do You Know?
- Word Problems
- Skill Up!
- SEE Learning

5E Learning Model

Engage · Explore · Explain · Extend · Evaluate

Adherence to National Education Policy

21st Century Skills (21 CS)

Learning Skills
- Critical Thinking
- Creativity and Innovation
- Collaboration
- Communication

Life Skills

Literacy Skills
- Information Literacy
- Media Literacy
- Technology Literacy

- Art Integration (AI)
- Cross Curricular (CC)
- India Focus (IF)
- Happiness Quotient (HQ)
- Experiential Learning (EL)

SUSTAINABLE DEVELOPMENT GOALS

Each feature has been tagged with colour-coded icons to easily identify the type of skills and learning being addressed!

About the Features

Interesting information and activities to connect maths with Indian history, art, culture, real-life situations and financial literacy

Chapter starter in the form of a picture-based exercise

Hands-on activity to help in improving investigation, reinforcement and extension of concepts just learnt

A variety of questions catering to inquiry-based, discovery-based, discussion-based and analysis-based learning

Picture-based, fun, problem-solving questions to reinforce concepts

Questions to stimulate rational thinking using mathematical skills

Special stories to promote social, emotional and ethical learning

Model making or hands-on project ideas to enhance learning beyond the classroom

Sample test papers at the end of the book for additional practice (Classes 6 to 8 Assessment Corner based on the New Assessment format)

Brief write-ups on eminent mathematicians and their contributions

Informative colourful posters to focus on some important concepts or facts

Contents

21 CS · Creativity and innovation, Communication · AI · EL · IF

MATHS IN INDIAN DRAWINGS

Warli painting is a tribal art practised by a tribe from Maharashtra called 'Warli' (or Varli). These paintings were traditionally made on the walls of huts of the villagers during festive seasons and on special occasions. They paint day-to-day activities of the people in the village. These activities include hunting, farming, dancing, celebrating festivals, etc. To draw the complete village scene, they also draw trees, rivers, houses and animals. Nowadays, you can easily find this art form on clothes, cushion covers, mobile covers, jewellery, etc.

Shapes and Patterns in Warli Paintings

This art form is drawn with simple shapes, **squares, circles and triangles,** where each shape has its own meaning. These shapes are repeated to form a continuous pattern.

The basic shapes used in Warli paintings have the following meaning:

- **Circle:** Represents the sun and the moon.
- **Triangle:** Represents trees, hills and mountains.
- **Square:** Represents an enclosed area or a piece of land.

Human and animal bodies are represented by two triangles joined at the tip, with circle for head and bent lines for hands and legs.

Warli prints and paintings are auspicious for the tribal people. Therefore, these are not used on any kind of footwear.

Create your own Warli painting in the space provided below. Show scenes from your daily life using the shapes and figures of life form.

You can use the following steps to create your own figures of life form.

Describe your painting in three sentences.

_____

_____

_____

LEARNING OBJECTIVES

- To compare different quantities
- To learn position words

LET'S GET STARTED

Tick (✔) the pictures having more objects in each row.

1.

2.

Top and Bottom

The clock is at the **top** of the cupboard.
The plant is at the **bottom** of the cupboard.

Tall and Short

Tia is **taller** than Raj.
Raj is **shorter** than Tia.

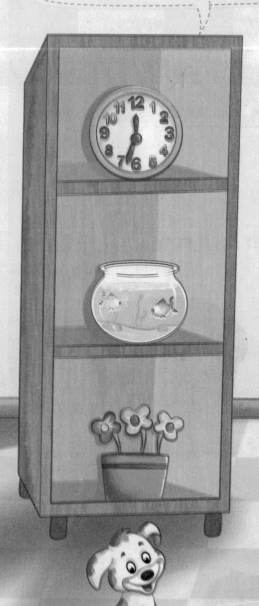

Tia

Raj

Near and Far

The cat is **near** the red ball.
The dog is **far** from the red ball.

Inside and Outside

The toys are **inside** the cupboard.

The ball is **outside** the cupboard.

Above and Below

Look at the bunk bed.
Mansi is **above** Preeti.
Preeti is **below** Mansi.

Mansi

Amit

Preeti

Riya

Dev

Behind and In front of

Riya is standing **behind** the curtain.
Amit is standing **in front of** the curtain.

On and Under

The flower vase is **on** the table.
Dev is hiding **under** the table.

Left and Right
The T-shirt is to the **left** of the towel.
The skirt is to the **right** of the towel.

Pia

T-shirt

Towel

Skirt

Jia

Heavy and Light
Jia is **heavier** than the soccer ball.
The soccer ball is **lighter** than Jia.

Big and Small
The cat is **bigger** than the kittens.
The kittens are **smaller** than the cat.

Before, After and Between

Ram is **before** Harleen.
Sana is **after** Harleen.
Harleen is **between** Ram and Sana.

Long and Short

The branch is **longer** than the caterpillar.
The caterpillar is **shorter** than the branch.

Up and Down

Mark is going **up** on the seesaw.
Aman is going **down** on the seesaw.

A. **Fill in the blanks with the help of the following words.**

on	under	near	far

1. The apples are kept ___on___ the table.
2. Reena stays ___near___ my house.

My house   *Reena's house*   *Peter's house*

3. Peter's house is ___far___ from my house.
4. The ball is lying ___under___ the table.

B. **Look at the pictures and fill in the blanks with the help of the given words.**

up	down	before	after	between

1. Aman is climbing ___up___ the steps.
2. Kriti is sliding ___down___ the slide.
3. Harry is standing ___after___ Fiza.
4. Ali is standing ___before___ Fiza.
5. Fiza is standing ___between___ Harry and Ali.

poof 13/6

WORKSHEET 1

H·W

Read, draw and colour.

1. The 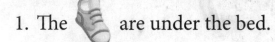 are under the bed.

2. The 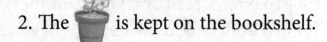 is kept on the bookshelf.

3. The is near the cat.

4. The is to the right of the lamp.

5. The is to the left of the lamp.

6. The is inside the jar.

15

LEARNING OBJECTIVES

- To count, read and write numbers from 1 to 20
- To understand the concept of zero
- To understand the place value of numbers from 1 to 20
- To identify numbers that come before, after and in between
- To understand increasing and decreasing orders
- To learn how to compare numbers
- To learn how to place numbers on the number line

LET'S GET STARTED

O N E, One
The sky has one shining sun.

T W O, Two
She is wearing two blue shoes.

T H R E E, three
Do you see three traffic lights?

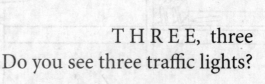

F O U R, Four
Four are the corners of the door.

F I V E, Five
Use your five fingers and let us high-five.

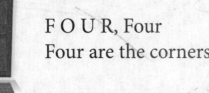

Build Your Own Rhyme!

Using the following hints, write your own rhyme for numbers 6 to 10.

Six-Sticks, Seven-Driven, Eight-Wait, Nine-Mine, Ten-Hen

NUMBERS FROM 1 TO 9

Numbers from 1 to 9 are single-digit numbers.

Number	Number Name	Representation
1	One	★
2	Two	★★
3	Three	★★★
4	Four	★★★★
5	Five	★★★★★
6	Six	★★★★★★
7	Seven	★★★★★★★
8	Eight	★★★★★★★★
9	Nine	★★★★★★★★★

CONCEPT OF ZERO

There are two plates in the kitchen. Compare the number of cookies in the two plates.

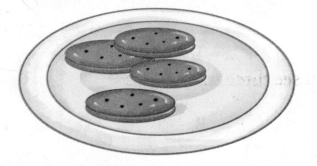 

There are four cookies on one plate. How many cookies are there on the other plate? NONE!

ZERO means absence of something.

Therefore, we have zero cookies on the other plate.

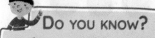 **Do you know?**
Other words used for zero are nil, none, nothing and naught.

1. **Colour as many fruits to match the numbers given for each box.**

a.

9

b.
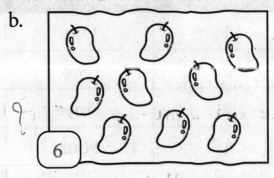
6

2. **Count the number of objects and circle the correct number.**

a.

0   1   2   ③   ④

b.

④   5   6   7   8

c.

5   6   7   8   ⑨

d.

5   6   ⑦   8   ⑨

3. **Match the following.**

a.

A.
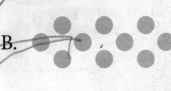

b.

B.

c.

C.

d.

D.

Ten, 10

Ten is the first two-digit number and it is written as 10.

We represent its quantity as ★★★★★★★★★★

PLACE VALUE

Numbers from 1 to 9 are single-digit numbers. They are written in the ones place. 10 is a two-digit number. We use '1' and '0' to represent 10.

The number 10 and all the other two-digit numbers are placed under tens and ones as shown below. This is called a **place value chart**.

Tens	Ones
1	0

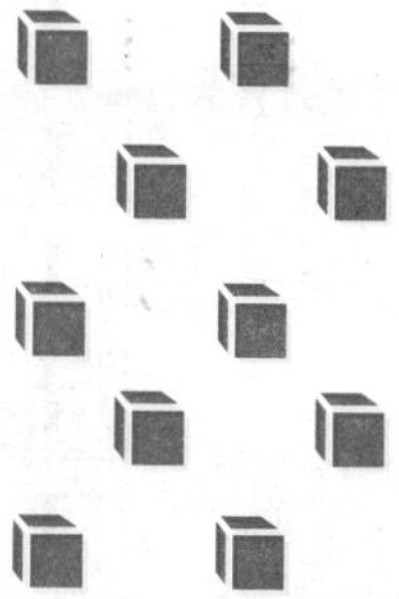

10 ones = 1 ten

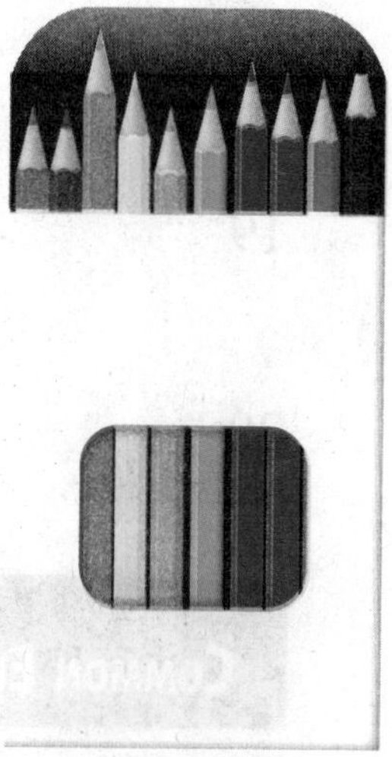

10 ones = 1 ten

Thus, 10 has 1 ten and 0 ones.

NUMBERS FROM 11 TO 20

Till now we have learnt numbers from 0 to 10. We will now learn numbers from 11 to 20.

Number	Name	Quantity	T	O
11	Eleven	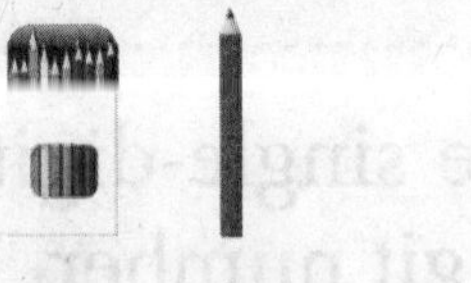	1	1
12	Twelve	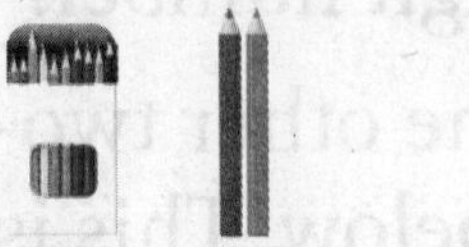	1	2
13	Thirteen	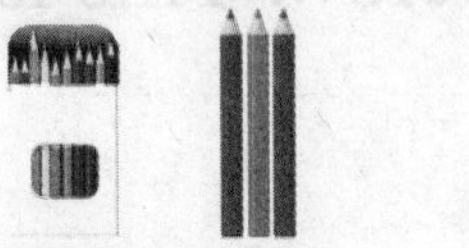	1	3
14	Fourteen	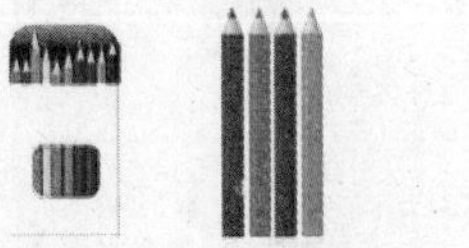	1	4
15	Fifteen	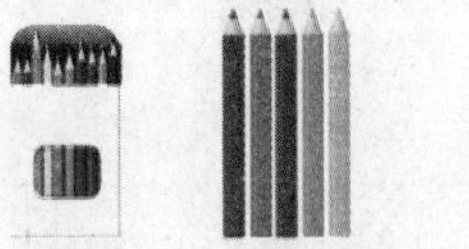	1	5
16	Sixteen	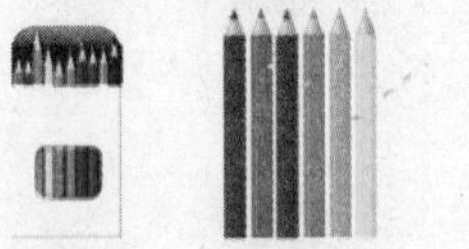	1	6
17	Seventeen	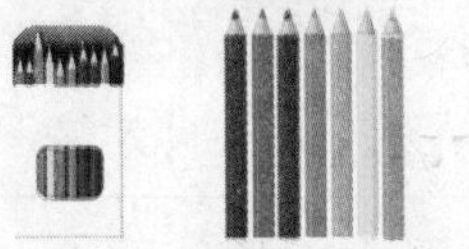	1	7
18	Eighteen	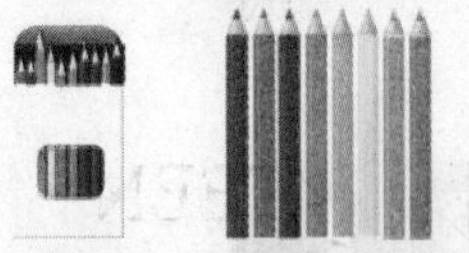	1	8
19	Nineteen	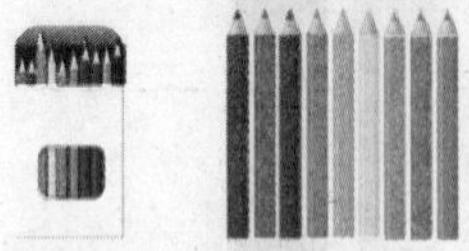	1	9
20	Twenty	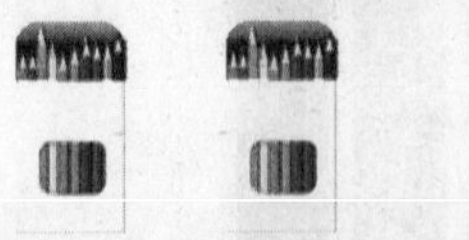	2	0

COMMON ERRORS

4	fore 👎	four 👍	13	threeteen 👎	thirteen 👍
14	foreteen 👎	fourteen 👍	15	fiveteen 👎	fifteen 👍
18	eightteen 👎	eighteen 👍			

20

EXERCISE 2B

1. Read aloud and write again in the given space.

Number	Number Name	Number	Number Name
11	ELEVEN	11	eleven
12	TWELVE	12	twelve
13	THIRTEEN	13	thirteen
14	FOURTEEN	14	fourteen
15	FIFTEEN	15	fifteen
16	SIXTEEN	16	sixteen
17	SEVENTEEN	17	seventeen
18	EIGHTEEN	18	eighteen
19	NINETEEN	19	nineteen
20	TWENTY	20	twenty

2. Count the number of pictures and fill in the blanks.

		Number	Number Name
a.		11	Eleven
b.		13	thirteen
c.		15	fifteen
d.		17	seventeen
e.		14	fourteen

3. Make a group of 10 objects and write the number. One has been done for you.

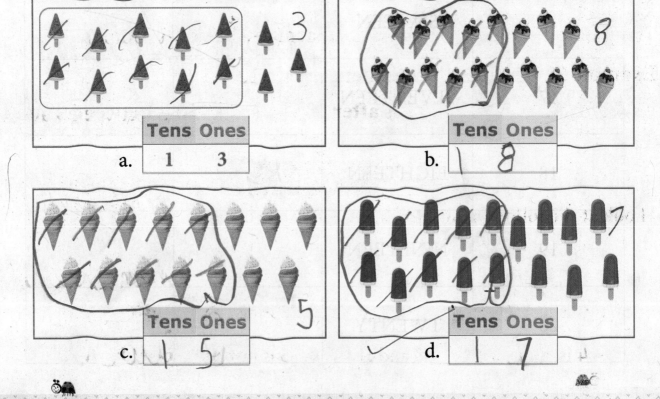

a.

Tens	Ones
1	3

b.

Tens	Ones
1	8

c.

Tens	Ones
1	5

d.

Tens	Ones
1	7

BEFORE, AFTER AND BETWEEN

The bike is parked **before** the car.

The car is parked **between** the bike and bicycle.

The bicycle is parked **after** the car.

Example 1: Look at the picture given below. Where is the football placed?

The football is placed between the alarm clock and the books.

Example 2: Consider the numbers. 9 10 11

9 is **before** 10. 11 is **after** 10. 10 is **between** 9 and 11.

EXERCISE 2C

Look at the following numbers and fill in the blanks.

3 4 5 ~~after, between before~~

1. 4 is just _after_ 3.

2. 5 is just _after_ 4.

3. 4 is _between_ 3 and 5.

4. 3 is just _before_ 4.

COMPARING NUMBERS

Crego, the crocodile, likes eating greater numbers. Always remember him while comparing numbers.

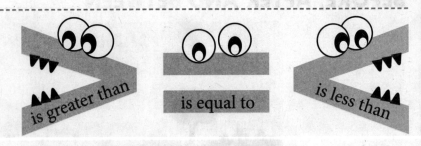

is greater than   is equal to   is less than

Symbols for 'Greater than' and 'Less than'

Compare 5 and 2.

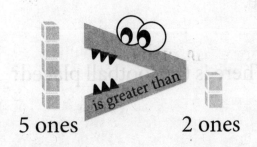

is greater than

5 ones   2 ones

5 is greater than 2. It is written as 5 > 2.

Compare 7 and 12.

is less than

7 ones   1 ten and
                2 ones

7 is less than 12. It is written as 7 < 12.

NOTE

The mouth of crocodile opens towards the greater number and closes towards the smaller number.

Compare 13 and 18.

First, compare the tens digits. They are equal (that is, 1).

Now, we compare the ones digits. 8 is greater than 3. Therefore, 18 is greater than 13.

DO YOU KNOW?

A two-digit number is greater than a one-digit number.

Tens	Ones		Tens	Ones
1	8	>	1	3

Symbol for 'Equal to'

The sign for **equal to** is =.

5 is equal to 5 is written as

$$5 = 5$$

is equal to

5   5

24

INCREASING ORDER AND DECREASING ORDER

In increasing order, we write numbers from the smallest to the greatest. Increasing order is also known as **ascending order**.

In decreasing order, we write numbers from the greatest to the smallest. Decreasing order is also known as **descending order**.

Example 3: Write the following numbers in increasing order.

a.

| 5 | 8 | 3 | 1 | 9 |

Solution:

1   3   5   8   9

Smallest number   Greatest number

b.

| 16 | 10 | 18 | 12 | 19 |

Solution:

10   12   16   18   19

Smallest number   Greatest number

Example 4: Write the following numbers in decreasing order.

Solution:

| 6 | 9 | 1 | 7 | 3 |

9   7   6   3   1

Greatest number   Smallest number

Go Easy!

Remember that ascend means to move upwards and descend means to move downwards.

NUMBER LINE

A number line is a straight line on which numbers are marked at equal gaps. The number line usually starts from zero(0). The value of the numbers increases as we move towards the right side. Similarly, the value of numbers decreases as we move towards the left side.

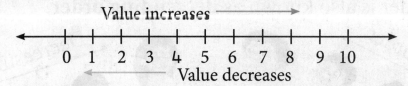

In a number line, a number on the left is less than the number on the right. For example, 4 is on the left of 5. So, 4 is less than 5.

A number on the right is greater than the number on the left. 5 is on the right of 4. So, 5 is greater than 4.

PUZZLE!

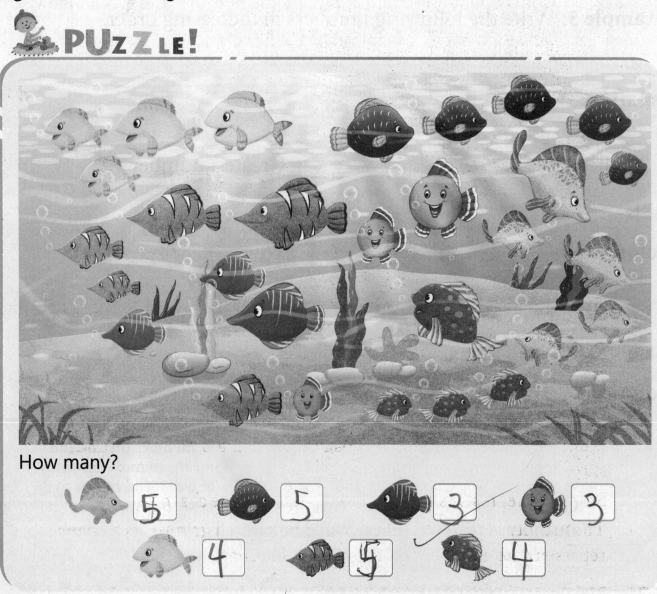

How many?

1. **Write the following in increasing and decreasing orders.**
   a. 19, 5, 7, 1, 6   1, 5, 6, 7, 9   19, 7, 6, 5, 1
   b. 15, 18, 13, 17, 11   11, 13

2. **Write >, < or =.**
   a. 5 < 9   b. 12 > 10   c. 19 > 11 ✓

3. **Colour the box with the greatest number in red and the box with the smallest number in yellow.**
   a. 2   9   6   7   b. 15   11   19   12

4. **Write the missing numbers to complete the number line given below.**
   a.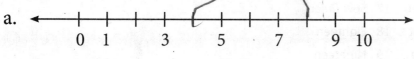
   0   1   3   5   7   9   10
   b.
   0   1   5   6   10

MATHS LAB ACTIVITY   21 CS   Critical thinking, Collaboration

Aim: To understand the concept of grouping in tens and comparing numbers
Materials required: Pebbles, plastic bags, number cards from 1 to 20
Procedure:
1. Arrange the students into groups of 4. Ask the groups to collect 20 pebbles each.
2. Student 1 of the first group picks up a number card, say 12.
3. Student 2 takes out the same number of pebbles, 12.
4. Student 3 fills the plastic bag with 10 pebbles and the remaining pebbles are left loose. For example, for 12, one bag should contain 10 pebbles and 2 pebbles should be left loose.
5. Student 4 represents the number on a place value chart in his/her notebook.
6. The activity is repeated till each student of each group gets a chance to represent the numbers on the place value chart.

Concept Map

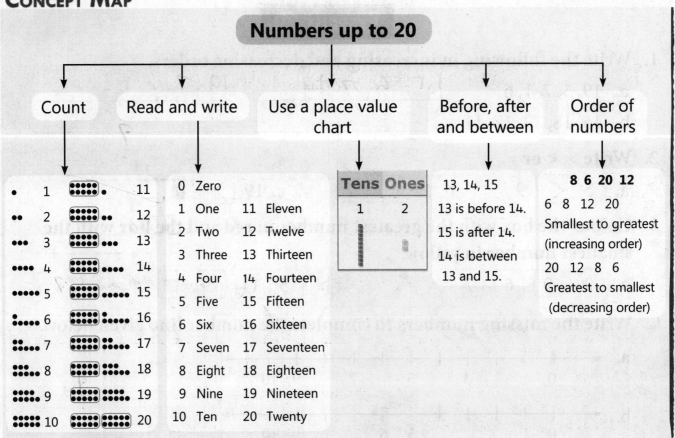

Numbers up to 20

- Count
- Read and write
- Use a place value chart
- Before, after and between
- Order of numbers

Count

1	11
2	12
3	13
4	14
5	15
6	16
7	17
8	18
9	19
10	20

Read and write

0	Zero		
1	One	11	Eleven
2	Two	12	Twelve
3	Three	13	Thirteen
4	Four	14	Fourteen
5	Five	15	Fifteen
6	Six	16	Sixteen
7	Seven	17	Seventeen
8	Eight	18	Eighteen
9	Nine	19	Nineteen
10	Ten	20	Twenty

Use a place value chart

Tens	Ones
1	2

Before, after and between

13, 14, 15

13 is before 14.

15 is after 14.

14 is between 13 and 15.

Order of numbers

8 6 20 12

6 8 12 20
Smallest to greatest (increasing order)

20 12 8 6
Greatest to smallest (decreasing order)

Key Concepts

- **Zero:** Zero represents the absence of something. It is written as 0.

- **Smallest:** The number which is the least in value

- **Greatest:** The number which is the most in value

- **Greater than:** Number with bigger value between the two numbers

- **Less than:** Number with smaller value between the two numbers

- **Equal to:** Numbers having the same value

- **Number line:** A straight line on which numbers are marked at equal gaps; the value of numbers increases as we move towards the right side and decreases as we move towards the left side.

- **Increasing order or ascending order:** The order in which the numbers are arranged from the smallest to the greatest

- **Decreasing order or descending order:** The order in which the numbers are arranged from the greatest to the smallest

CHAPTER REVISION

A. Write the number and the number name for the following items.

		Number	Number Name
1.	✿✿✿	3	three
2.	✿✿✿✿✿	5	five
3.	✿✿✿✿✿✿✿✿✿✿	10	ten
4.	✿✿✿✿✿✿✿✿✿✿✿✿✿✿✿✿	16	sixteen
5.	✿✿✿✿✿✿✿✿✿	9	nine

B. Write the following numbers in increasing and decreasing orders.

1. 19, 1, 8, 15, 12   1, 8, 12, 15, 19,   19, 15, 12, 8, 1
2. 5, 20, 13, 8, 16   5, 8, 13, 16, 20,   20, 16, 13, 8, 5

C. Write the number as directed.

Just before   Just after   Between
 16 17   6 7   12 13 14

D. Write >, < or =.

1.

2.

E. Colour the box with the greatest number in red and the box with the smallest number in yellow.

1. 10 16 17 7   2. 7 20 13 4

SKILL UP!

A.

21 CS   Information literacy

How many members are there in your family? Write down the total count in your notebook. Compare the same with your classmates.

B.

21 CS   Critical thinking, Life skills

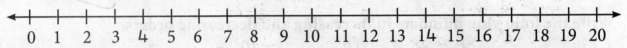

Akash and Aman helped their father by watering the plants. Aman watered 16 plants. Akash watered 10 plants.
Who watered more number of plants?

Do you also help your parents? Is it important to grow plants? How does it help our environment?

C.

21 CS   Critical thinking

Look at the number line given below.

0 1 2 3 4 5 6 7 8 9 10 11 12 13 14 15 16 17 18 19 20

If you skip one number after 1 and continue till 20, what numbers will you stop at?

Complete the number line accordingly.

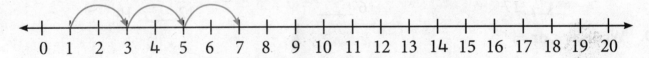

0 1 2 3 4 5 6 7 8 9 10 11 12 13 14 15 16 17 18 19 20

SUSTAINABLE DEVELOPMENT GOALS

What do you think would make our world and our planet a better place? What can you do to make it better? There is a list of 17 goals that can help in making the world and our planet better. These goals are called the Sustainable Development Goals adopted by the United Nations in 2015. You can participate in each goal, even in a small way and do something for the world and our planet. One such small step is growing more plants. Growing more plants would help in making life on land better. Question B is related to SDG 15 Life on Land.

H-W

Look at these beautiful flowers and butterflies in a garden.

A. Count the number of flowers and butterflies and write the numbers in the boxes.

 2   2

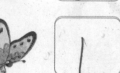 3   1

 1   6

B. Which one is the greatest in number? Circle the correct picture.

3 Addition up to 20

LEARNING OBJECTIVES

- To add numbers up to 20 and study addition facts
- To learn addition using number line
- To learn different number combinations
- To add two 1-digit numbers, and add 1-digit and 2-digit numbers
- To learn how to add three numbers
- To solve word problems on addition

LET'S GET STARTED

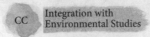 CC Integration with Environmental Studies 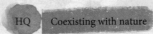 HQ Coexisting with nature

Asif and Ravi are celebrating the Earth day. They are cleaning the park by collecting the garbage. Radha, Anna and Riya also join them. These three girls start watering the saplings. So, there are two boys and three girls in the park now. How many children are there in all? Would you like to join them too? Why should we water the plants?

ADDING TWO NUMBERS

Riya and Soham went to the beach with their parents. While walking alongside the beach, Riya collected 4 seashells. Soham collected 3 seashells. Let us find out the total number of seashells that they have collected.

Seashells collected by Riya

Seashells collected by Soham

We know that 4 is greater than 3. To know the total number of seashells, we can count forward from the greater number which is 4.

3 more than 4

$$4 \; 5 \; 6 \; 7$$

$$4 + 3 = 7$$

This is read as four plus three is equal to seven.

So, Riya and Soham collected 7 seashells.

We can change the order of numbers in addition.

For example, the total number of frogs can be calculated as:

$$3 + 2 = 5$$

or

$$2 + 3 = 5$$

Therefore, when we count all the frogs, we see that there are 5 frogs in all.

The result of addition remains the same when numbers are added in any order.

ADDITION FACTS

Adding 0 to a Number

There are two nests.
One nest has 0 eggs. Another nest has 3 eggs.
How many eggs are there in all?

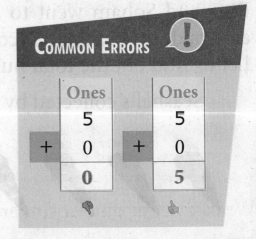

| 0 eggs | + | 3 eggs | = | **3 eggs** |

Similarly,

| 2 fish | + | 0 fish | = | **2 fish** |

> **When 0 is added to a number, the answer is the number itself.**

Adding 1 to a Number

Rakhi ate 2 toffees. Later she ate 1 more toffee. How many toffees did Rakhi eat?

$$2 \quad + \quad 1 \quad = \quad 3$$

When we add 1 to 2, we get the number just after it, that is 3.

Rahil has 4 yellow markers. He buys 1 blue marker. How many markers does he have in all?

$$4 \quad + \quad 1 \quad = \quad 5$$

When we add 1 to 4, we get the number just after it, that is 5.

> **When 1 is added to a number, the answer is the number just after it.**

Vertical Addition of Two 1-digit Numbers

Numbers can also be added vertically by writing one number below the other.

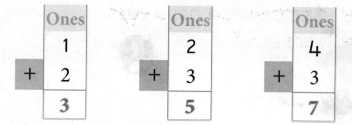

We can count on our fingers too.

$$3 + 2 = ?$$

Count 3 and 2 on your fingers. Look at the dots marked on the hand. The total number of dots are

$$3 + 2 = 5$$

Example 1: There are 4 ducklings on the ground. There are 2 ducklings in the pond. How many ducklings are there in all?

Solution: Number of ducklings on the ground = 4

Number of ducklings in the pond = 2

Adding the numbers, we get

$$4 + 2 = \boxed{}$$

4, 5, $\boxed{6}$

Go Easy!

While adding, it is better to start with the greater number.

So, there are 6 ducklings in all.

35

Add the following.

1.

   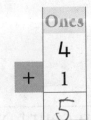

4   +   1   =

Ones
4
+ 1
5

2.

5   +   2   =

Ones
5
+ 2
7

3.

3   +   4   =

Ones
3
+ 4
8

4.

6   +   2   =

Ones
6
+ 2
8

5.

6   +   3   =

Ones
6
+ 3
9

ADDITION USING NUMBER LINE

Let us add two numbers on a number line.

Help the frog to take 5 + 2 steps.

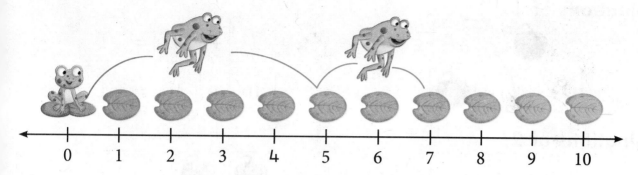

To add 5 and 2, the frog begins from 0 and moves 5 places to the right. Next, it moves 2 more places to the right. The frog reaches 7. Thus, **5 + 2 = 7.**

Go Easy!

To add on the number line, always move to the right.

Example 2: Add 4 and 5 using the number line.

Solution: To add 4 and 5, we begin from 0 and move 4 places to the right. Next, move 5 more places to the right. We reach 9.

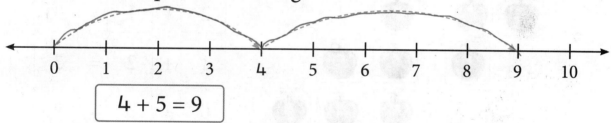

$$4 + 5 = 9$$

Example 3: Solve 5 + 4 on the number line.

Solution: To add 5 and 4, we begin from 0 and move 5 places to the right. Next, move 4 more places to the right. We reach 9.

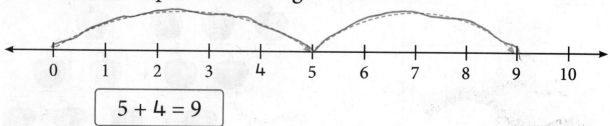

$$5 + 4 = 9$$

Here, we again observe that when numbers are added in any order, the answer is the same.

That is, 4 + 5 = 5 + 4 = 9

NUMBER COMBINATIONS

Any number can be represented as a combination of numbers. These are called number combinations. Let us look at some number combinations.

Combinations of 1

🎃 + ☐

☐ + 🫑

| 1 | + | 0 | = | 1 |
| 0 | + | 1 | = | 1 |

Combinations of 2

2	+	0	=	2
1	+	1	=	2
0	+	2	=	2

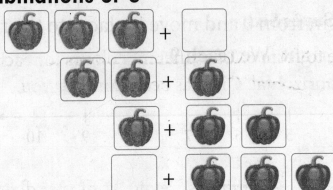

Combinations of 3

3	+	0	=	3
2	+	1	=	3
1	+	2	=	3
0	+	3	=	3

Combinations of 4

4	+	0	=	4
3	+	1	=	4
2	+	2	=	4
1	+	3	=	4
0	+	4	=	4

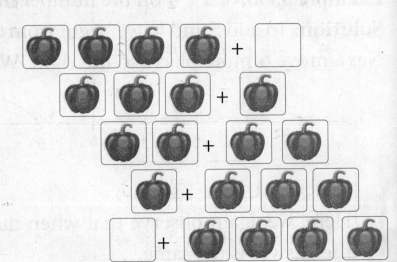

Combinations of 5

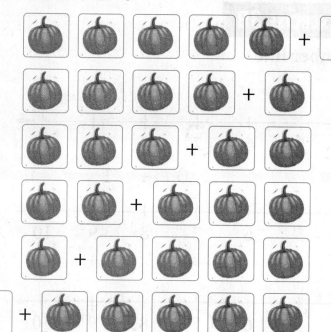

5	+ 0 =	5
4	+ 1 =	5
3	+ 2 =	5
2	+ 3 =	5
1	+ 4 =	5
0	+ 5 =	5

CROSSWORD

Super Six!

Circle two numbers that combine to form 6. Use different colours for each set. These sets can be vertical or horizontal. One has been done for you.

Super Six

2	4	1	3	3
3	5	1	2	3
3	4	1	4	2
0	6	5	3	0
4	2	4	3	6
1	5	3	4	2
5	2	1	3	4

Do you know?
Dominoes are blocks or tiles divided into two equal parts with a line in the middle. Each part is marked with a few spots or is blank.

39

1. Solve the following on the number line.

a. 4 + 3

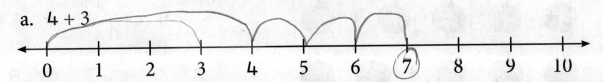

b. 1 + 3

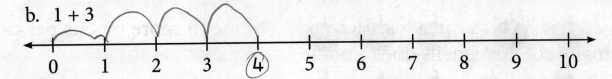

c. 2 + 5

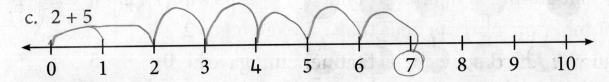

d. 5 + 4

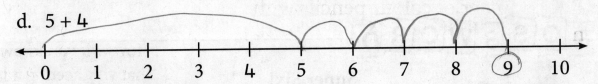

e. 3 + 6

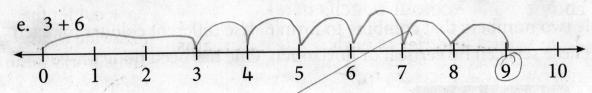

2. Fill in the missing numbers using number combinations.

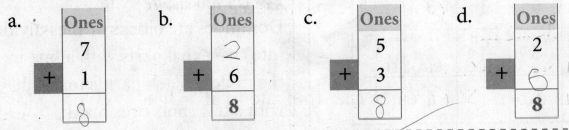

a.

Ones
7
+ 1
8

b.

Ones
2
+ 6
8

c.

Ones
5
+ 3
8

d.

Ones
2
+ 6
8

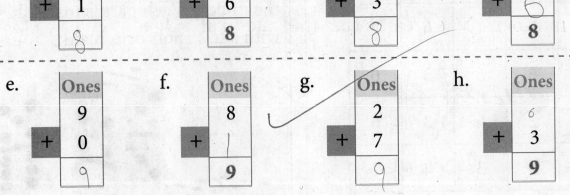

e.

Ones
9
+ 0
9

f.

Ones
8
+ 1
9

g.

Ones
2
+ 7
9

h.

Ones
6
+ 3
9

WORD PROBLEMS ON ADDITION

Word problems are the mathematical problems that are expressed entirely in words. The problems can be based on real-life situations. You need to read and understand the sentences describing the real-life situation. Then you can solve the problem by way of a mathematical calculation.

Example: Read the following real-life situation.

Thoihen has 2 colour pencils. Her aunt gave her 5 more colour pencils. How many colour pencils does Thoihen have in all?

Let us find out the total number of colour pencils with Thoihen.

The number of colour pencils that Thoihen has = 2

The number of colour pencils that her aunt gave her = 5

So, the total number of colour pencils with
Thoihen = 2 + 5
= 7

Thus, Thoihen has 7 colour pencils in all.

Example 4: Reena and her friends ate 4 ice creams in the morning and 1 ice cream in the evening. How many ice creams did they have in all?

Solution: The number of ice creams that Reena and her friends ate in the morning = 4

The number of ice cream that they ate in the evening = 1

So, the number of ice creams that they ate in all = 4 + 1
= 5

4 ice creams   + 1 ice cream

Ones
4
+ 1
5

Reena and her friends ate 5 ice creams in all.

Go Easy!

How will you know that you need to add? Look out for the following words. These words mean addition.

- In all
- In total
- Altogether

1. **Meena has 1 red crayon. John has 2 green crayons. How many crayons do they have in total?**

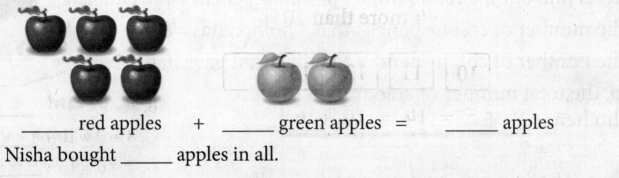

_____ red crayon   +   _____ green crayons =   _____ crayons

They have _____ crayons in total.

2. **Nisha bought 5 red apples and 2 green apples. How many apples did Nisha buy in all?**

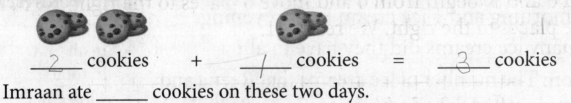

_____ red apples   +   _____ green apples =   _____ apples

Nisha bought _____ apples in all.

3. **Imraan ate 6 cookies on Monday. He ate 3 cookies on Tuesday. How many cookies did he eat on these two days?**

__2__ cookies   +   __1__ cookies   =   __3__ cookies

Imraan ate _____ cookies on these two days.

4. **4 butterflies are flying. 2 more join them. How many butterflies are flying in all?**

__4__ butterflies   +   __2__ butterflies   =   __6__ butterflies

There are __6__ butterflies flying in all.

ADDING TWO 1-DIGIT NUMBERS TO GIVE A 2-DIGIT NUMBER

Let us add 6 and 5. Count forward 5 from 6.

6   Counting forward, we get 11

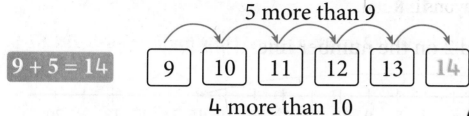

5 more than 9

$9 + 5 = 14$

| 9 | 10 | 11 | 12 | 13 | 14 |

4 more than 10

$10 + 4 = 14$

| 10 | 11 | 12 | 13 | 14 |

$$9 + 5 = 14 = 10 + 4$$

MENTAL MATHS

A. $5 + 6 = 10 +$ _____
B. $4 + 8 = 10 +$ _____
C. $8 + 7 = 10 +$ _____
D. $7 + 6 = 10 +$ _____

Addition on Number Line

Solve 6 + 5 on the number line.

To add 6 and 5, begin from 0 and move 6 places to the right. Next, move 5 more places to the right. We reach 11.

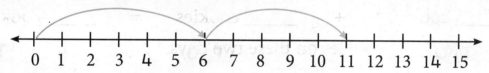

ADDING 2-DIGIT AND 1-DIGIT NUMBERS

Steps to follow:

1. Group the numbers into tens and ones.   2. Add the ones.
3. Add the tens.

Example 5: Solve 12 + 5.

Solution: Write 12 as 1 ten and 2 ones.
Write 5 under 2. Add the ones digits. $5 + 2 = 7$
We get 7 in the ones place and 1 in the tens place.
So, $12 + 5 = 17$.

T	O
1	2
+	5
1	7

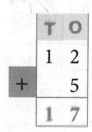

Example 6: Add the following numbers.

a.   13 and 6 b.   15 and 3

Solution:

a.
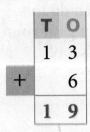

b.
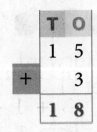

COMMON ERRORS !

T	O
1	0
+ 1	
2	**0**
👎

T	O
1	0
+	1
1	**1**
👍

Example 7: Add 15 and 2 on the number line.

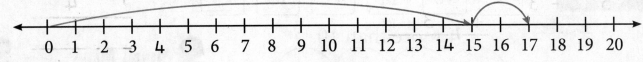

Therefore, 15 + 2 = 17.

EXERCISE 3D

1. **Add the following numbers.**

a.
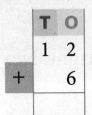

b.
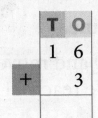

c.
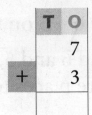

d.
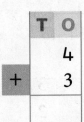

e.
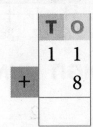

f.
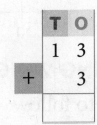

2. **Add the following numbers on the number line.**

a. 6 + 3

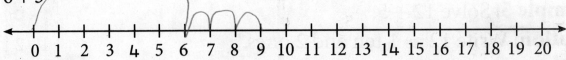

b. 12 + 5

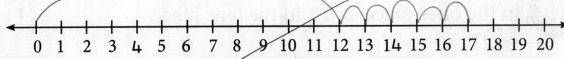

ADDING THREE NUMBERS

To add three numbers, first add two numbers and then add the third number to the sum of the first two numbers. This addition can be done horizontally or vertically.

Example: Add 4, 1 and 3.

Horizontally   Vertically

4 + 1 + 3

4 + 1 + 3

5   + 3

8

4
5
1   **8**
+   3

8

First add 4 and 1.
$4 + 1 = 5$
Then add 5 and 3.
$5 + 3 = 8$

Horizontally   Vertically

4 + 1 + 3

4 +   4

8

3
4
1   **8**
+   4

8

First add 1 and 3.
$1 + 3 = 4$
Then add 4 and 4.
$4 + 4 = 8$

> **The result of addition remains the same when the numbers are added either horizontally or vertically.**

EXERCISE 3E

Add the following numbers.

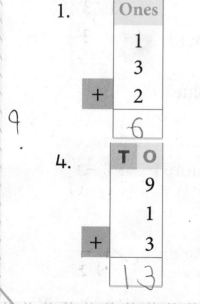
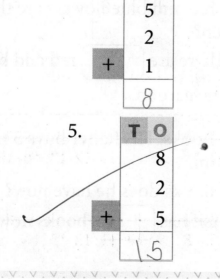

1.
Ones
1
3
+ 2
6

2.
Ones
5
2
+ 1
8

3.
Ones
3
2
+ 4
9

4.
T	O
	9
	1
+	3
1	3

5.
T	O
	8
	2
+	5
1	5

6.
T	O
	7
	4
+	3
1	4

WORD PROBLEMS

I have 5 muffins.

Then I buy 5 more.

How many muffins do I have now?

I have 10 muffins.

T	O
	5
+	5
1	0

EXERCISE 3F

1.

   Rajiv has a packet of 10 marbles. He buys 6 more marbles.

   How many marbles does Rajiv have now?

   Solution: Rajiv has ⟨16⟩ marbles now.

T	O
1	0
	6
+	
1	6

2.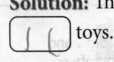

   Anil has 7 toy cars. Sunil has 4 toy buses.

   How many toys do the two boys have together?

   Solution: The two boys together have ⟨11⟩ toys.

T	O
1	7
+	4
1	1

3. There are 15 red flowers and 2 blue flowers in a garden.

   How many red and blue flowers are there in the garden?

   Solution: There are ⟨17⟩ red and blue flowers in the garden.

T	O
1	5
	2
+	
1	7

4. Asif has 14 books. His father buys 5 more books for him.

   How many books does he have now?

   Solution: Asif has ⟨19⟩ books now.

T	O
1	4
	5
+	
1	9

Aim: Developing the concept of addition using number blocks

Materials required: Number blocks, number cards (numbers from 1 to 10)

Procedure:

1. Arrange the students into groups of 4.
2. Student 1 of the first group picks two number cards, say 4 and 9.
3. Student 2 picks the same number of blocks, 4 and 9.
4. Student 3 adds the blocks to get the total number of blocks.
5. Student 4 keeps the record in his/her notebook as:

Card 1		Card 2		Total
4	+	9	=	13
6	+	5	=	11

6. Students can exchange the roles in the next turn and continue with this activity till each student of each group gets a chance to add the number blocks.

CONCEPT MAP

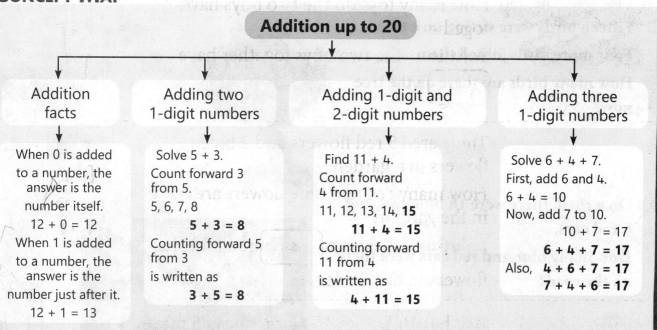

Addition up to 20

Addition facts

When 0 is added to a number, the answer is the number itself.
$12 + 0 = 12$
When 1 is added to a number, the answer is the number just after it.
$12 + 1 = 13$

Adding two 1-digit numbers

Solve $5 + 3$.
Count forward 3 from 5.
5, 6, 7, 8
$5 + 3 = 8$
Counting forward 5 from 3
is written as
$3 + 5 = 8$

Adding 1-digit and 2-digit numbers

Find $11 + 4$.
Count forward 4 from 11.
11, 12, 13, 14, **15**
$11 + 4 = 15$
Counting forward 11 from 4
is written as
$4 + 11 = 15$

Adding three 1-digit numbers

Solve $6 + 4 + 7$.
First, add 6 and 4.
$6 + 4 = 10$
Now, add 7 to 10.
$10 + 7 = 17$
$6 + 4 + 7 = 17$
Also, **$4 + 6 + 7 = 17$**
$7 + 4 + 6 = 17$

KEY CONCEPTS

- **Adding:** Putting two or more numbers (or things) together to get the total quantity
- We can add numbers in any order.

A. Add the following.

1.
T	O
1	4
+	2
1	**6**

2.
T	O
1	8
+	0
1	**8**

3.
T	O
1	1
+	7
1	**8**

4.
T	O
	8
+	5
1	**3**

5.
T	O
5	
8	
+	2
1	**5**

6.
T	O
7	
3	
+	2
1	**2**

B. Add 6 and 7 on the number line.

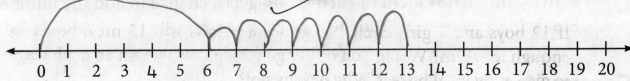

0 1 2 3 4 5 6 7 8 9 10 11 12 13 14 15 16 17 18 19 20

C. Fifteen birds were sitting on a tree.

Four more birds joined them.

How many birds are there on the tree now?

T	O
1	5
+	4
1	**9**

D. On a road, there were 14 blue cars and 4 red cars.

How many blue and red cars were there on the road?

T	O
1	4
+	4
1	**8**

Skill up!

A.

Take a number, say 8. Look for the domino number card that has a total of 8 on it, that is 4 and 4, 6 and 2, 5 and 3, etc.

Repeat the same procedure with different numbers and write down the number combinations in your notebook.

B.

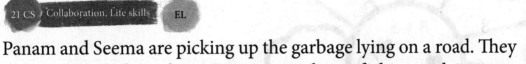

Panam and Seema are picking up the garbage lying on a road. They pick up 5 polythene bags, 3 empty packets of chips and 1 empty bottle. How many items did they pick up in all? Should we throw garbage on the road? Give reasons for your answer.

C.

If 12 boys and 7 girls decide to go for a picnic, will 15 meal boxes be enough for them? Would you rather go for a picnic or visit an orphanage to give away meal boxes? Why or why not?

SUSTAINABLE DEVELOPMENT GOALS

Question B is related to SDG 13 Climate Action and SDG 15 Life on Land. If we do not throw garbage at a proper place, it will make the land dirty and lead to climate change. So, think about what you can do to keep our land clean and help in stopping climate change.

Worksheet 3

21 CS | Critical thinking | AI

Add the numbers and colour as per the given colour codes.

Colour codes:

5 = Red	8 = Sky blue	9 = Orange
10 = Yellow	11 = Green	12 = Pink

4 Subtraction up to 20

- To understand the meaning of subtraction
- To learn about ways to subtract and the subtraction facts
- To subtract numbers using the number line
- To subtract 1-digit numbers from 2-digit numbers
- To solve word problems on subtraction

LET'S GET STARTED

It is Amit's birthday today. His friends are visiting his place. He decides to help his mother by placing cookies on a plate. While placing them on the plate, he finds that some of the cookies are not in good condition.

5 cookies

2 crumbled cookies

Cookies in good condition?

How many cookies are in good condition? _____3_____

INTRODUCTION TO SUBTRACTION

Amit buys 7 candies. He eats 3 candies. Let us find out the number of candies that are left with Amit.

As Amit eats 3 out of 7 candies, we cross out 3 candies.

He is left with 4 candies now.

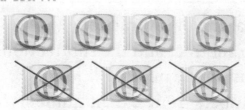

We can also write this as

$$7 - \overset{3}{4} = \overset{4}{3}$$

> We use the symbol '−', read as 'minus', to subtract numbers.

This is read as 'Seven minus ~~four~~ three is equal to three'.

Example 1: 9 − 1 = ___8___

Solution: 9 − 1 means we take away 1 from 9.

$$9 - 1 = 8$$

NOTE

Crossing out means taking away.

VERTICAL SUBTRACTION

Like addition, we can also subtract using the vertical method. In subtraction, we place the greater number above the smaller number.

Examples:

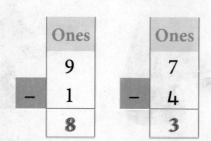

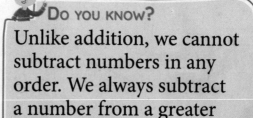

DO YOU KNOW?
Unlike addition, we cannot subtract numbers in any order. We always subtract a number from a greater number.

> Subtraction is taking away things. When we subtract a number from a given number, the given number becomes smaller.

Cross out to subtract. One has been done for you.

1. | 5 | − | 2 |

	Ones
	5
−	2
	3

2. | 5 | − | 1 |

	Ones
	5
−	1
	4

3. | 8 | − | 3 |

	Ones
	8
−	3
	5

4. | 7 | − | 2 |

	Ones
	7
−	2
	5

5. | 9 | − | 4 |

	Ones
	9
−	4
	5

6. | 7 | − | 6 |

	Ones
	7
−	6
	1

7. | 8 | − | 4 |

	Ones
	8
−	4
	4

WAYS TO SUBTRACT

Counting Forward to Subtract

Example 2: There are 8 birds on a branch. Five of them fly away. How many birds are still sitting on the branch?

Solution: Start from the smaller number, 5. Count forward to reach 8.

3 steps

| 5 | 6 | 7 | 8 |

You took 3 steps.

Therefore, 8 – 5 = **3**

Counting Backwards to Subtract

Example 3: Roy has 8 apples. He gives 2 apples to Tom. How many apples are left with Roy?

Solution:

Start from the bigger number, 8.

Count backwards by 2 numbers.

You took 2 steps.

Therefore, 8 – 2 = **6**

GO EASY!

We always count backwards from the bigger number.

2 steps

| 6 | 7 | 8 |

EXERCISE 4B

1. Count forward to subtract. One has been done for you.

a.
Ones
7
– 2
5

2, 3, 4, 5, 6, ⑦

b.
Ones
5
– 2
3

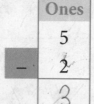

c.
Ones
6
– 4
2

4, 5, 6

2. Count backwards to subtract. One has been done for you.

a.
③, 4, 5, 6, 7

Ones
7
– 4
3

b.
Ones
9
– 7
2

c.
Ones
5
– 4
1

SUBTRACTION FACTS

Subtracting 0 from a number

There are three frogs in a pond.

None of them jumps out of the pond.

How many frogs are there in the pond?

Zero frogs jumped out of the pond.

Therefore,

$$3 - 0 = 3$$

MENTAL MATHS

Solve.

A. $3 - 0 = $ _3_

B. $5 - 0 = $ _5_

C. $9 - 0 = $ _9_

One frog jumps out of the pond.

We have,

$$3 - 1 = 2$$

Now, one more frog jumps out of the pond.

$$3 - 2 = 1$$

Subtracting a Number from Itself

There are three frogs in the pond. All the frogs jump out of the pond. How many frogs are there in the pond?

All the frogs jumped out of the pond.

Therefore,

$$3 - 3 = 0$$

Zero shows absence of something.

SUBTRACTION ON THE NUMBER LINE

Subtract 3 from 8.

The bee is at 8.

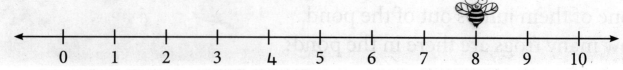

It will take 3 jumps towards the left to reach 5.

Therefore,

$$8 - 3 = 5$$

> To subtract on the number line, we always move to the left (except while subtracting zero).

PUzZle!

Look at the number above the domino. How many more dots are needed to get that number?

7

4

6

3

Example 4: Solve 4 – 1 on the number line.

Solution: 1 is to be subtracted from 4. So, start from 4 and jump 1 place to the left. We will reach 3.

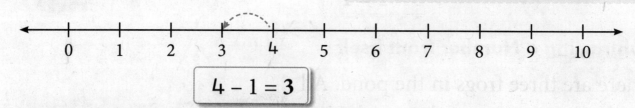

$$4 - 1 = 3$$

Example 5: Solve 7 – 0 on the number line.

Solution: As 0 is to be subtracted from 7, we will not move leftwards on the number line.

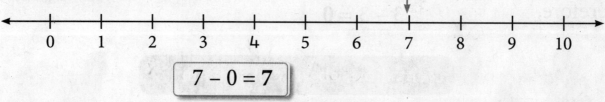

$$7 - 0 = 7$$

1. **Subtract the following on the number line.**

   a. 5 – 3 = 2

   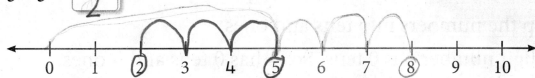

   b. 4 – 2 = 2

   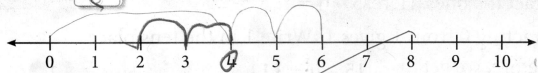

   c. 7 – 1 = 6

   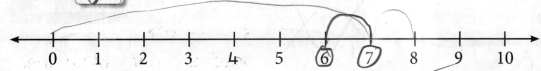

   d. 8 – 0 = 8

   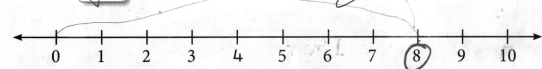

2. **Subtract the following.**

   a. 5 – 0 = 5   b. 6 – 1 = 5   c. 9 – 0 = 9

   d. 4 – 1 = 3   e. 4 – 0 = 4   f. 7 – 0 = 7

3. **Subtract and match. One has been done for you.**

   a. 8 – 2   3   6 – 1

   b. 6 – 2   2   9 – 3

   c. 10 – 5   4   5 – 2

   d. 9 – 6   5   8 – 4

   e. 3 – 1   6   6 – 4

SUBTRACTION OF 1-DIGIT NUMBERS FROM 2-DIGIT NUMBERS ....

A fruit seller has 15 bananas. He sells 4 bananas to Jack. How many bananas are left with the fruit seller?

Steps to follow:

1. Group the numbers into tens and ones.

2. A 1-digit number has 0 tens. So, 4 has 0 tens and 4 ones.
   15 has 1 ten and 5 ones.

	T	O
	1	5
−	0	4
	1	1

3. Subtract the ones. Here, $5 - 4 = 1$.

4. Subtracting 0 from 1 gives 1. Write 1 in the tens place.
   Therefore, we get $\boxed{15 - 4 = 11}$

Examples:

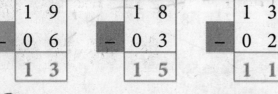

T	O
1	9
− 0	6
1	3

T	O
1	8
− 0	3
1	5

T	O
1	3
− 0	2
1	1

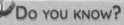

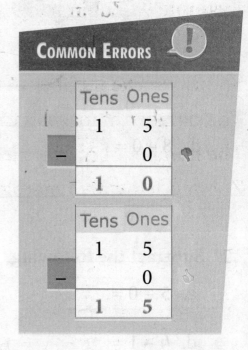

COMMON ERRORS

Tens	Ones
1	5
−	0
1	**0**

Tens	Ones
1	5
−	0
1	**5**

Do you know?

A set or a group of mathematical facts using the same numbers is called a fact family.
Thus, the numbers 2, 6 and 8 can be used to create the following facts.

Addition Facts: $6 + 2 = 8$ and $2 + 6 = 8$

Subtraction Facts: $8 - 2 = 6$ and $8 - 6 = 2$

WORD PROBLEMS

Example 6: I had 5 pencils. I gave 3 pencils to my friend. How many pencils do I have now?

Solution: The number of pencils I have = 5
The number of pencils I gave to my friend = 3
The number of pencils I have now = $5 - 3 = 2$
I have 2 pencils now.

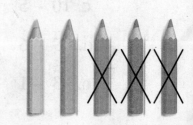

Example 7: Priya had 7 cupcakes. She ate 5 cupcakes.

How many cupcakes are left with Priya?

Solution: The number of cupcakes with Priya = 7

The number of cupcakes eaten by Priya = 5

The number of cupcakes left = 7 – 5 = 2

Priya is left with 2 cupcakes now.

Example 8: What is 3 less than 8?

$$8 - 3 = 5$$

Solution: 3 less than 8 is 5.

Example 9: Zubin had 9 marbles. He lost 4 marbles.

How many marbles are left with Zubin?

Solution: The number of marbles with Zubin = 9

The number of marbles that Zubin lost = 4

The number of marbles left with Zubin = 9 – 4 = 5

Zubin is left with 5 marbles now.

12/12/22

EXERCISE 4D

1. **Subtract the following.**

a.
T	O
1	2
–	1
1	1

b.
T	O
1	5
–	2
1	3

c.
T	O
1	6
–	4
1	2

d.
T	O
1	7
–	6
1	1

e.
T	O
1	8
–	5
1	3

f.
T	O
1	9
–	2
1	7

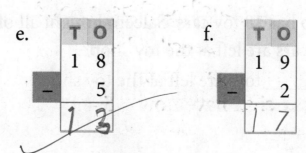

2. Answer the following.

a. There are 7 flowers in a flower vase. Susan took 3 flowers. How many flowers are left in the vase?

	T	O
	7	2
−	3	
		4

_____4_____ flowers are left in the vase.

b. Sumit bought 16 ice cream cones. He and his friends ate 4 ice creams. How many ice creams cones are left?

_____12_____ ice creams cones are left.

	T	O
	1	6
−		4
	1	2

c. Aarti has 12 flowers. Two of them are pink. Rest are blue. How many blue flowers are there ?

There are _____10_____ blue flowers.

	T	O
	1	2
−		2
	1	0

d. Harleen has 18 marbles. She gives 7 marbles to Dev. How many marbles are left with Harleen?

Harleen has _____11_____ marbles left with her.

	T	O
	1	8
−		7
	1	1

e. A toy shop has 18 toy cars. Saleem bought all of them. How many toy cars are left at the toy shop?

_____0_____ toys are left at the toy shop.

	T	O
	1	8
−	1	8
	0	0

Aim: To subtract numbers up to 20

Materials required: Number cards in a bowl, paper strip, pencil, clay

Procedure:

1. Arrange the students into groups of 4.
2. Student 1 of the first group takes out any number from the bowl, say 8.
3. Student 2 writes the number on a paper strip and rolls the same number of clay dough balls.
4. Student 3 takes out another number, say 5 and presses 5 clay dough balls.
5. Student 4 counts the number of unpressed balls and writes the subtraction statement on the paper strip as 8 – 5 = _____. Complete this subtraction statement.
6. The activity is repeated till every member of each group gets a chance to subtract numbers.

CONCEPT MAP

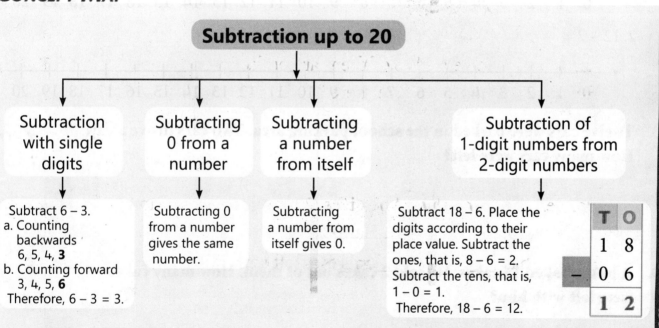

Subtraction up to 20

Subtraction with single digits	Subtracting 0 from a number	Subtracting a number from itself	Subtraction of 1-digit numbers from 2-digit numbers
Subtract 6 – 3. a. Counting backwards 6, 5, 4, **3** b. Counting forward 3, 4, 5, **6** Therefore, 6 – 3 = 3.	Subtracting 0 from a number gives the same number.	Subtracting a number from itself gives 0.	Subtract 18 – 6. Place the digits according to their place value. Subtract the ones, that is, 8 – 6 = 2. Subtract the tens, that is, 1 – 0 = 1. Therefore, 18 – 6 = 12.

T	O
1	8
– 0	6
1	**2**

KEY CONCEPTS

- **Subtraction:** To take away
- **Number Line:** A line on which numbers are given in an order
- We always subtract a number from a bigger number.

CHAPTER REVISION

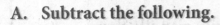

A. Subtract the following.

1.

T	O
1	2
–	1
1	1

2.

T	O
1	5
–	3
1	2

3.

T	O
1	6
–	2
1	4

4.

T	O
1	7
–	5
1	2

5.

T	O
1	8
–	3
1	5

6.

T	O
1	5
–	5
1	0

B. Subtract using the number line.

1. 18 – 9 = 9

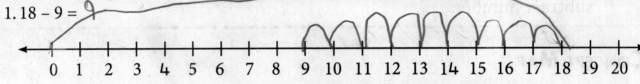

0 1 2 3 4 5 6 7 8 9 10 11 12 13 14 15 16 17 18 19 20

2. 12 – 7 = 5

0 1 2 3 4 5 6 7 8 9 10 11 12 13 14 15 16 17 18 19 20

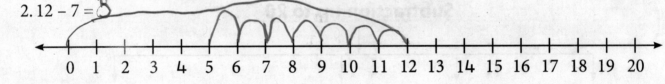

C. Twelve cars were parked in the school parking area. Two cars drove away. How many cars were left?

T	O
1	2
–	2
1	0

D. A baker baked 15 cakes. He sold 2 cakes out of them. How many cakes were left with him?

T	O
1	5
–	2
1	3

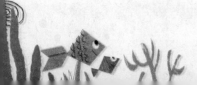

SKILL UP!

A. 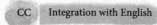 21 CS / Critical thinking, Communication   CC   Integration with English

Use the following number cards to frame subtraction problems or sentences. In each question or sentence, use each number card only once.

| 2 | 3 | 6 | 8 | 9 | 10 | − | = |

For example:

A tree has 8 yellow and green mangoes. Two mangoes are yellow. How many mangoes are green?

$$8 - 2 = 6$$

Write down more such questions or sentences using these number cards. Solve the questions as well.

B.  21 CS / Critical thinking, Life Skills

Harmeet was hungry. Ali had 7 oranges. He gave 2 oranges to Harmeet. Now Ali has ___5___ oranges. Ali shares his food with his friends all the time.

Do you take care of your friends? Why or why not? Is there any other way by which you can take care of your friends?

SUSTAINABLE DEVELOPMENT GOALS

Do you think sharing is important? Sharing would help the world in many ways. Sharing food would help in fighting hunger. This is related to SDG 2 Zero Hunger which is being addressed in Question B.

WORKSHEET 4

Decorate the Christmas tree by matching the correct answer and colour the shapes accordingly.

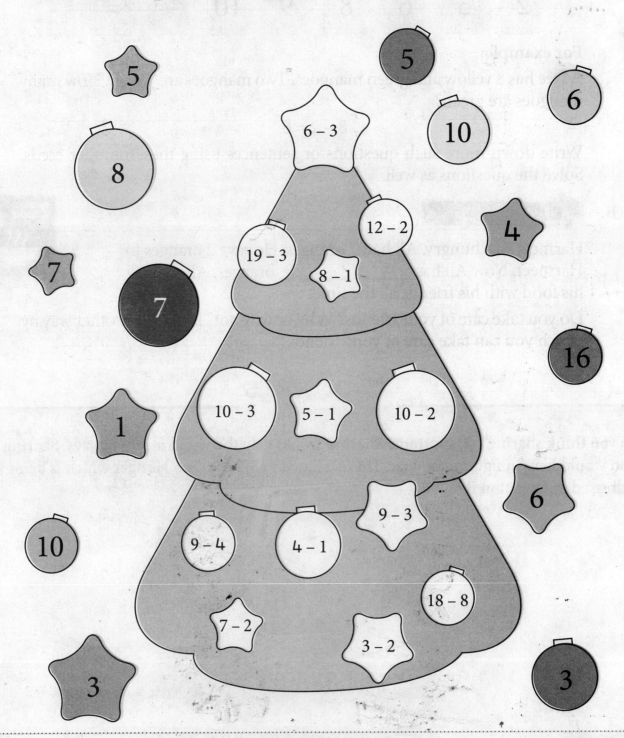

LEARNING OBJECTIVES

- To identify shapes and colours
- To identify objects having either the same shape or the same size or have the same shape and size
- To identify lines and curves
- To identify objects that are spheres or cubes
- To learn about rolling and sliding objects
- To identify patterns

LET'S GET STARTED   AI

Fill in the blanks with the names of the shapes. Colour the butterfly using these shapes and colour codes.

 = Square   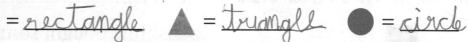 = rectangle   ▲ = triangle   ● = circle

SAME SHAPE

Ashima bought two story books. What do you notice about the shape of these story books?

Both are rectangles.
Both have different sizes.

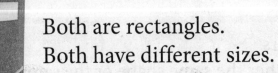 
SAME SIZE

Now have a look at these two books. What do you notice?

Both are rectangles.
Both have the same size.

SAME SHAPE AND SIZE

Ashima bought some cookies.
She ate the following two cookies.

What do you notice about the shape and size of these two cookies? These cookies have the same shape and size.

LINES AND CURVES

These are **straight lines**. These are **curved lines**.

Straight lines do not bend. Curved lines bend.

MENTAL MATHS

Find the following.
A. Letters with straight lines
B. Letters with curved lines

1. **Circle the shape having the same size as the given shape.**

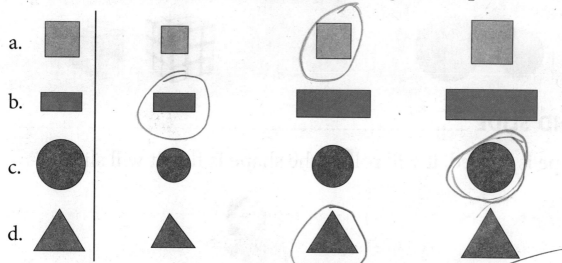

a.

b.

c.

d.

2. **Tick (✔) the figures that are of the same shape in each row.**

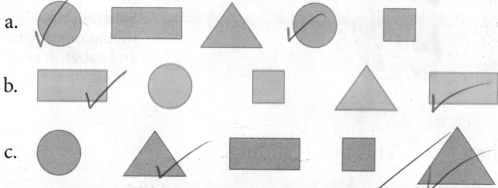

a.

b.

c.

3. **Circle the figures having the same shape and size as the given shape.**

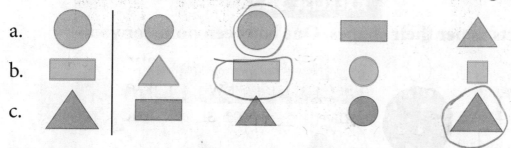

a.

b.

c.

4. **Trace over the dots with curved lines using a blue pencil and straight lines using a green pencil.**

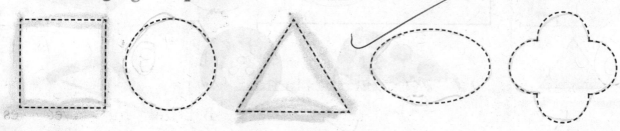

SORTING SHAPES

Sphere
Cube

ROLL AND SLIDE

If the shape is curved, it will roll. If the shape is flat, it will slide.

GO EASY!

Spheres show rolling movement and cubes show sliding movement.

This ball is rolling.   This box is sliding.

EXERCISE 5B

Sort the objects as per their shapes. One has been done for you.

PATTERNS

To make patterns, repeat what has come before.

In the following patterns, the marked shapes are repeated.

There is a change in size.

There is a change in colour.

1. Complete the following patterns by colouring.

2. Draw and colour the next two shapes in the given pattern.

3. What would be the next three shapes in the following pattern?

4. Study the patterns and circle the object that will come next.

a.

b.

Aim: To enable the students to make their own patterns

Materials required: Coloured tiles of different sizes, bowl

Procedure:

1. Arrange the students into groups of 3.
2. Student 1 of the first group takes out two tiles from the bowl.
3. Student 2 takes another two tiles and creates a pattern.
4. Student 3 identifies the pattern. He/she picks the shapes that are required to continue the pattern.
5. The group discusses the pattern.
6. Repeat the activity till every student of each group gets a chance to make a pattern.

CONCEPT MAP

Shapes and Patterns

Identifying shapes and lines

Basic shapes

Straight lines | Curved lines

Sphere | Cube
Some more shapes

Sorting

Same shape

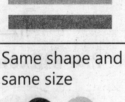

Same size

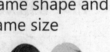

Same shape and same size

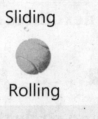
Sliding

Rolling

Making patterns

Change in size

Change in shape

Change in colour

Change in shape and colour

KEY CONCEPTS

- **Shapes:** The outline of a figure or an object
- **Size:** How big or small a shape or an object is
- **Straight line:** A long stretch in one direction that does not bend
- **Curved line:** Different from a line because it bends

A. Circle the shapes that are the same shape as the coloured shape. Colour the shapes as well.

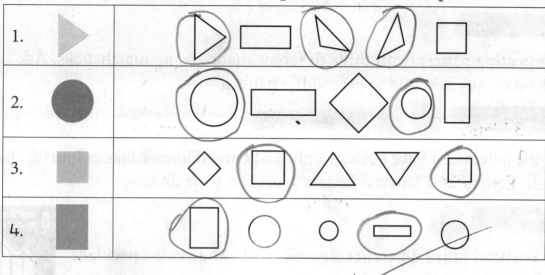

B. Colour the following.

1. Same shape and same size   2. Same shape

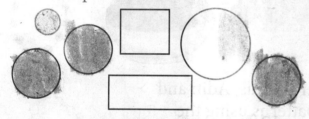   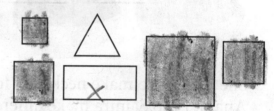

C. Circle the following.

1. Shapes with only curved lines

2. Shapes with only straight lines

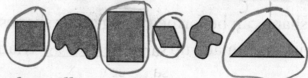

D. Study the pattern and circle the object that will come next.

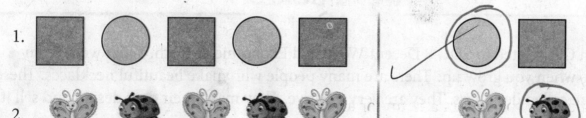

A. 21 CS / Creativity and innovation   EL

Make a repeating pattern with three different shapes using matchsticks. Ask your friends what comes next and to extend the pattern.

B. 21 CS / Critical thinking, Creativity and innovation   AI   CC   Integration with English

Find out the letters that have both straight and curved lines. Make colourful charts on 'Straight Letters' and 'Curved Letters' based on your finding.

C. 21 CS / Creativity and innovation, Life skills   EL

Samira has a bowl full of different coloured beads. She made a necklace using red and blue beads.

She decides to make necklaces for her friends, Aditi and Anam. Help Samira make different patterns using the coloured beads from the bowl.

Have you ever made things for your friends? If yes, how did that make you feel?

D. 21 CS / Critical thinking

A shape can be formed using other shapes.

This star is made up of _____ triangles.

SUSTAINABLE DEVELOPMENT **GOALS**

Question C is related to SDG 8 Decent Work and Economic Growth. What would you like to be when you grow up? There are many people who make beautiful necklaces. These people are called designers. They are very creative. They make their own design and sell it to earn money.

WORKSHEET 5

Identify and colour the pattern to help Little Red Riding Hood reach her grandma's home safely.

Grandma's home

Wolf

Red Riding Hood

2919122

LEARNING OBJECTIVES

- To learn numbers up to 100 in numerals and in words
- To learn expanded form of numbers
- To learn how to place numbers before, after and in between
- To compare numbers and understand greatest and smallest numbers
- To arrange numbers in increasing and decreasing orders
- To understand the method of skip counting

LET'S GET STARTED

How many? Write the number.

 5   7    8   15   4    3

COUNTING IN TENS

Ten sticks make one bundle.

29/9/22

10 sticks ⟶ 1 ten

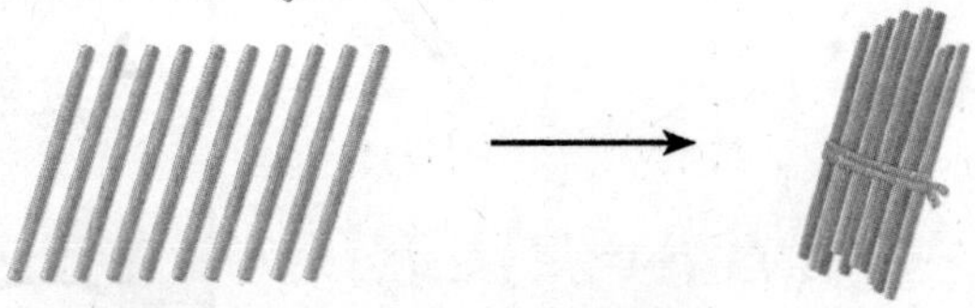

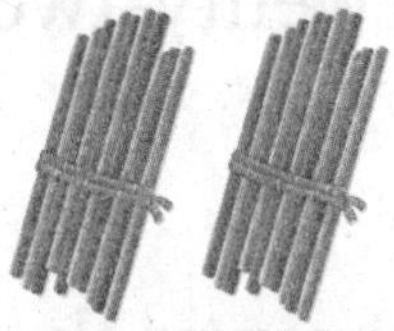

20 sticks = 2 tens (**Twenty**) 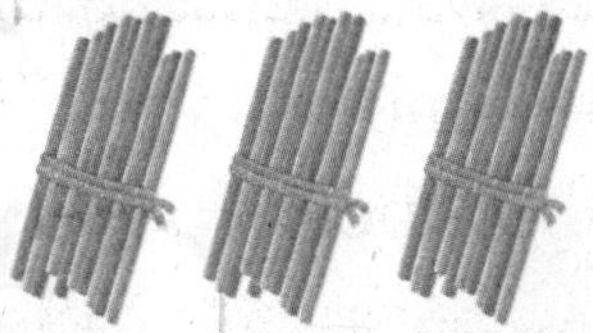 30 sticks = 3 tens (**Thirty**)  40 sticks = 4 tens (**Forty**)

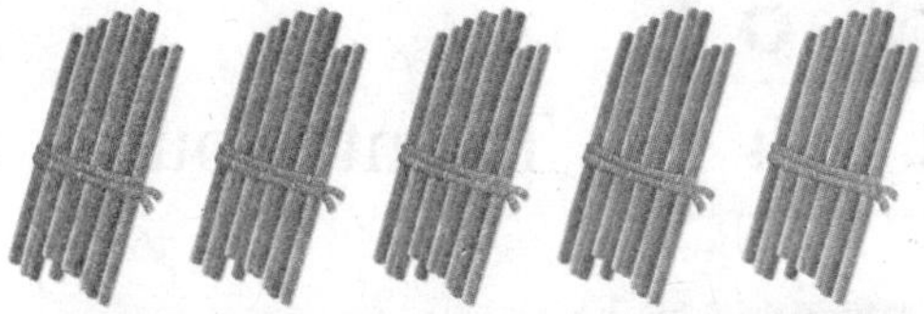

50 sticks = 5 tens (**Fifty**)  60 sticks = 6 tens (**Sixty**)

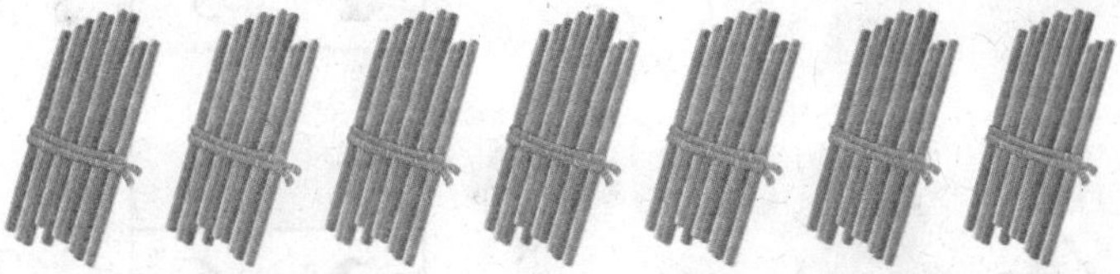

70 sticks = 7 tens (**Seventy**)

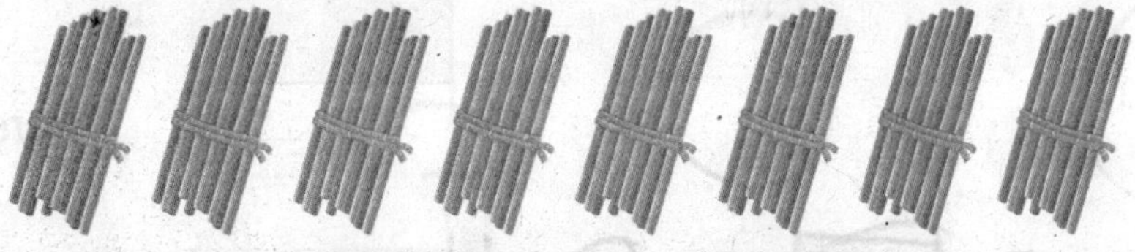

80 sticks = 8 tens (**Eighty**)

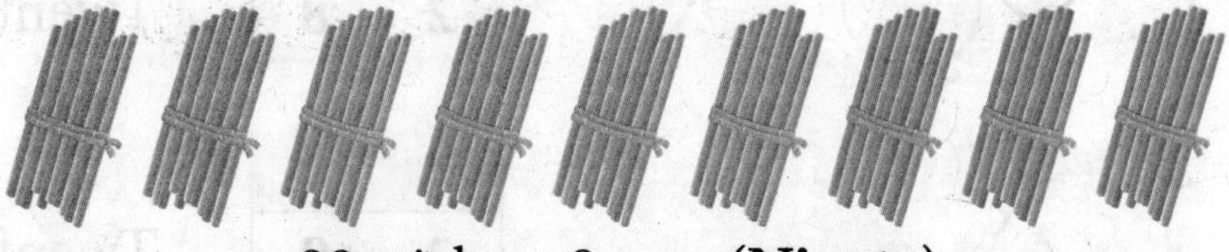

90 sticks = 9 tens (**Ninety**)

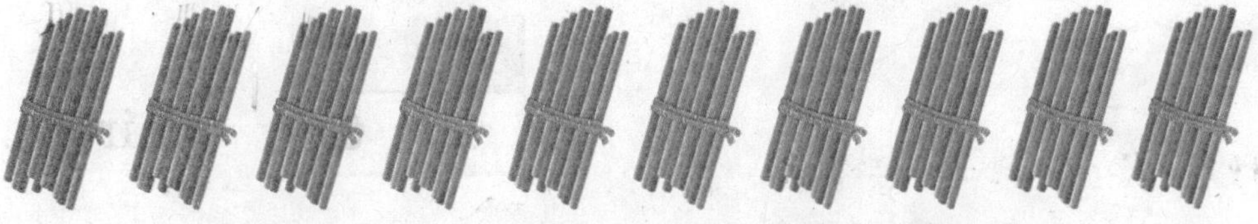

100 sticks = 10 tens (**One hundred**)

NUMBERS FROM 21 TO 30

T	O	
2	1	Twenty-one

T	O	
2	2	Twenty-two

T	O	
2	3	Twenty-three

T	O	
2	4	Twenty-four

T	O	
2	5	Twenty-five

T	O	
2	6	Twenty-six

T	O	
2	7	Twenty-seven

T	O	
2	8	Twenty-eight

T	O	
2	9	Twenty-nine

T	O	
3	0	Thirty

NUMBERS FROM 31 TO 40

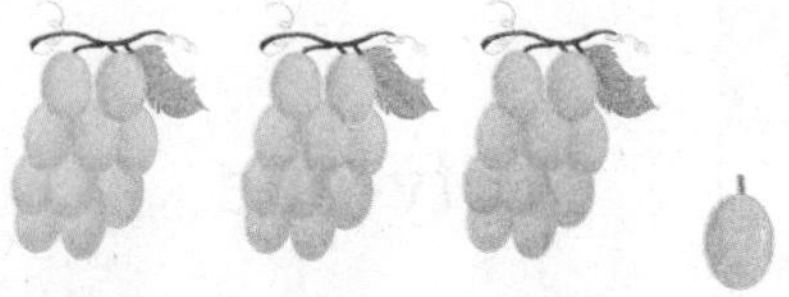

T	O
3	1

Thirty-one

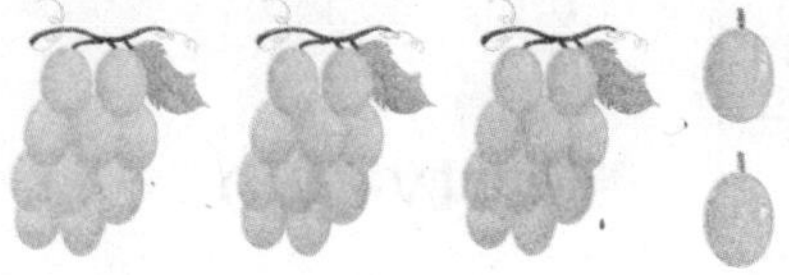

T	O
3	2

Thirty-two

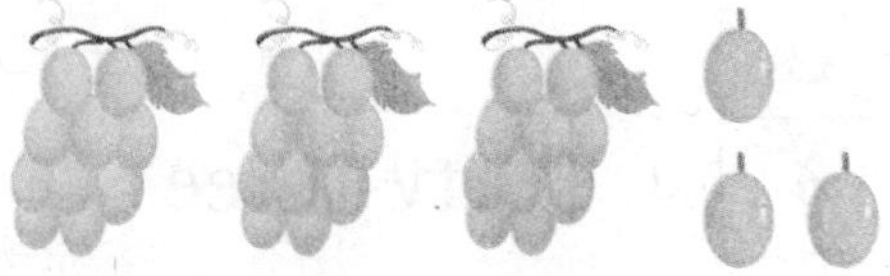

T	O
3	3

Thirty-three

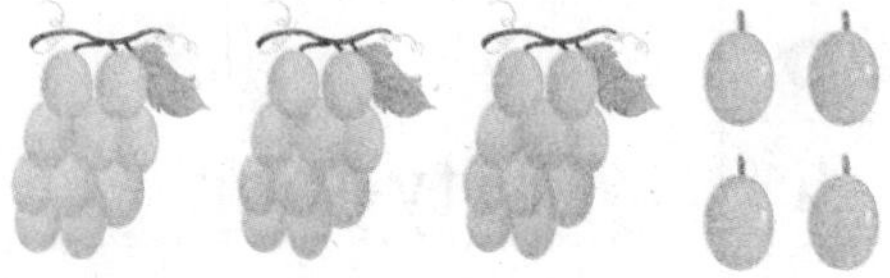

T	O
3	4

Thirty-four

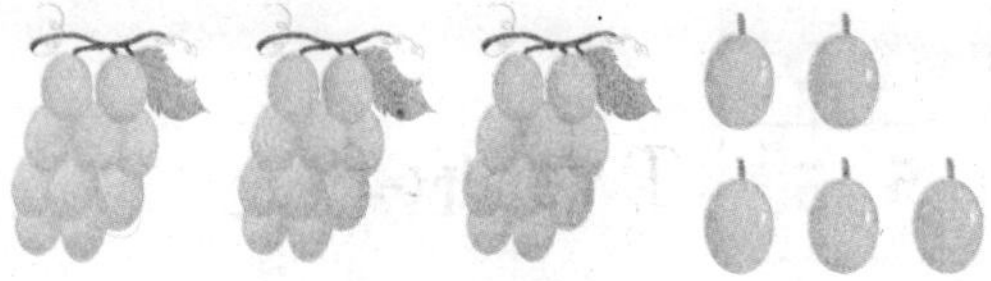

T	O
3	5

Thirty-five

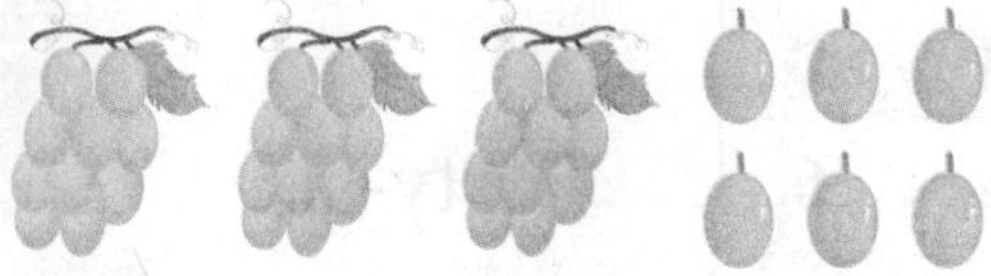

T	O
3	6

Thirty-six

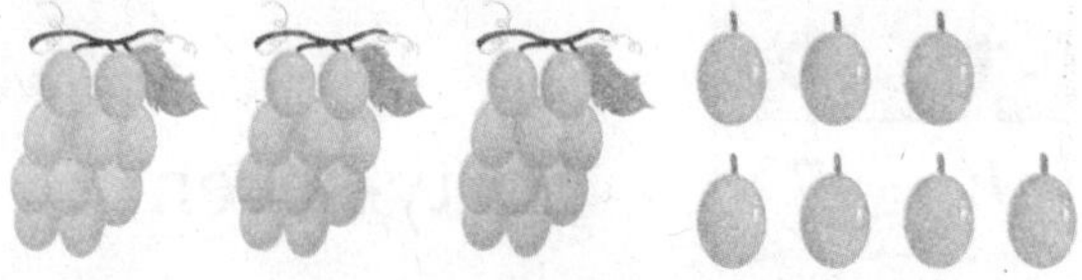

T	O
3	7

Thirty-seven

T	O
3	8

Thirty-eight

T	O
3	9

Thirty-nine

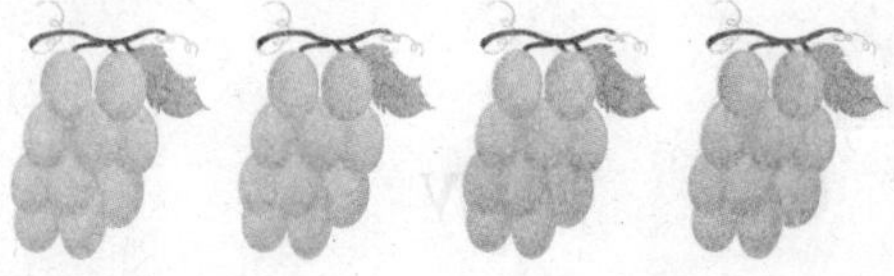

T	O
4	0

Forty

NUMBERS FROM 41 TO 50

2919122

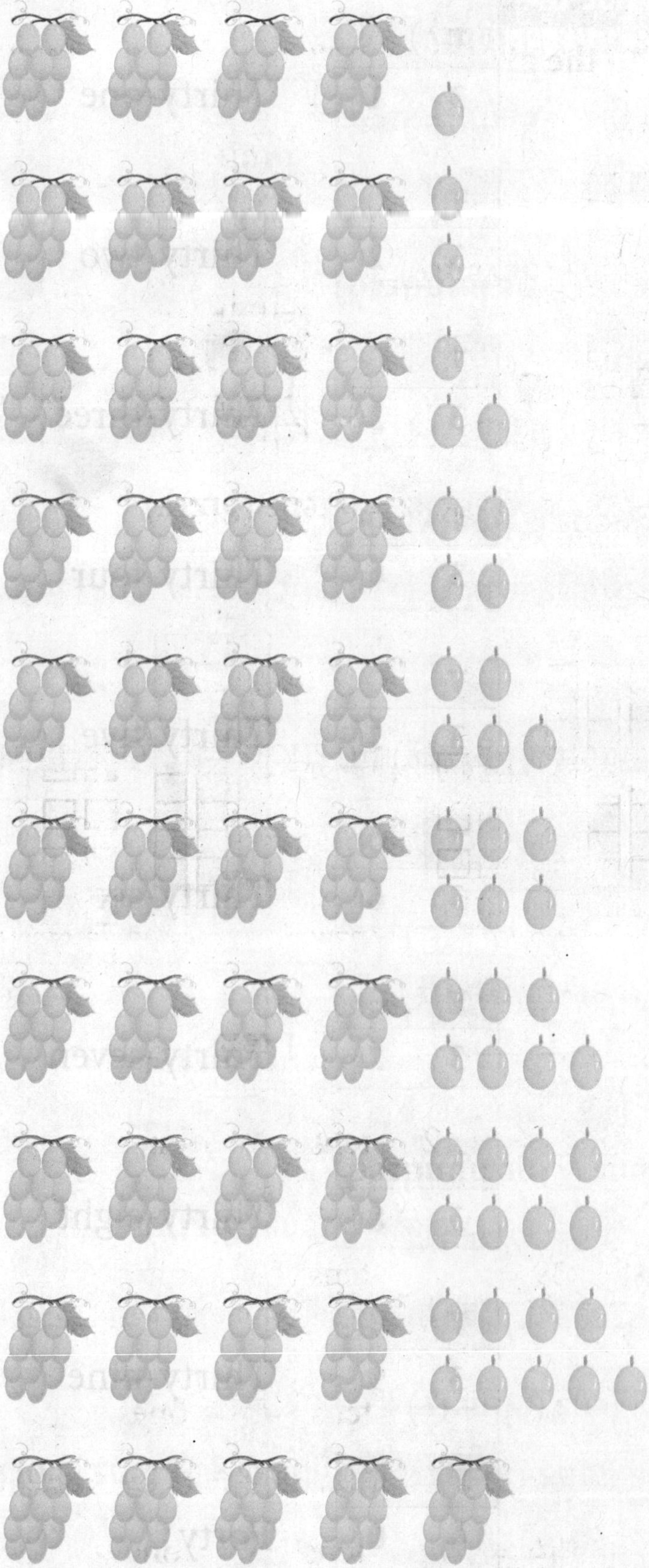

T	O
4	1

Forty-one

T	O
4	2

Forty-two

T	O
4	3

Forty-three

T	O
4	4

Forty-four

T	O
4	5

Forty-five

T	O
4	6

Forty-six

T	O
4	7

Forty-seven

T	O
4	8

Forty-eight

T	O
4	9

Forty-nine

T	O
5	0

Fifty

291922

EXERCISE 6A

1. Write the number corresponding to the given tens and ones.

a.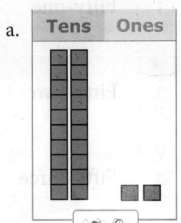

22

b.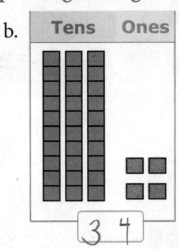

3 4

c.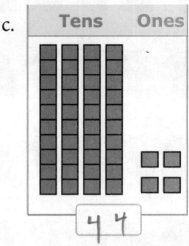

4 4

d.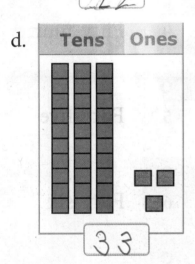

33

e.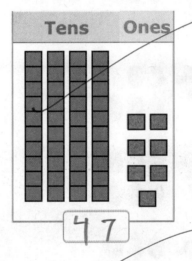

47

f.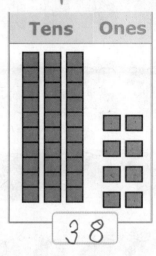

38

2. Fill in the blanks. One has been done for you.

a.

20 = [2] tens [0] ones

b.

39 = [3] tens [9] ones

c.

26 = [2] tens [6] ones

d.

44 = [4] tens [4] ones

NUMBERS FROM 51 TO 60 --

T	O
5	1

Fifty-one

T	O
5	2

Fifty-two

T	O
5	3

Fifty-three

T	O
5	4

Fifty-four

T	O
5	5

Fifty-five

T	O
5	6

Fifty-six

T	O
5	7

Fifty-seven

T	O
5	8

Fifty-eight

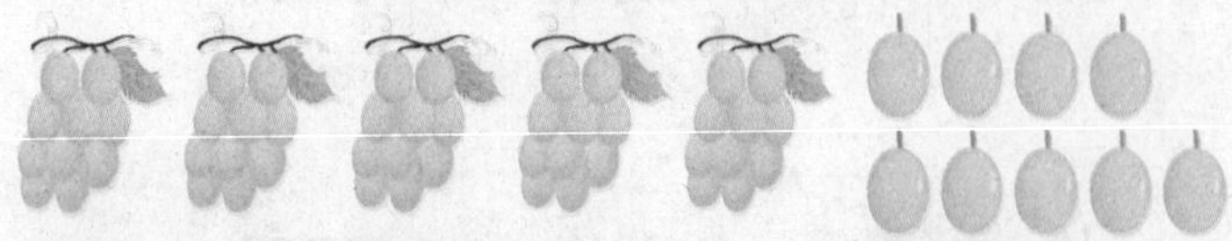

T	O
5	9

Fifty-nine

T	O
6	0

Sixty

NUMBERS FROM 61 TO 70

T	O	
6	1	Sixty-one

T	O	
6	2	Sixty-two

T	O	
6	3	Sixty-three

T	O	
6	4	Sixty-four

T	O	
6	5	Sixty-five

T	O	
6	6	Sixty-six

T	O	
6	7	Sixty-seven

T	O	
6	8	Sixty-eight

T	O	
6	9	Sixty-nine

T	O	
7	0	Seventy

NUMBERS FROM 71 TO 80

T	O	
7	1	Seventy-one

T	O	
7	2	Seventy-two

T	O	
7	3	Seventy-three

T	O	
7	4	Seventy-four

T	O	
7	5	Seventy-five

T	O	
7	6	Seventy-six

T	O	
7	7	Seventy-seven

T	O	
7	8	Seventy-eight

T	O	
7	9	Seventy-nine

T	O	
8	0	Eighty

NUMBERS FROM 81 TO 90

T	O	
8	1	Eighty-one

T	O	
8	2	Eighty-two

T	O	
8	3	Eighty-three

T	O	
8	4	Eighty-four

T	O	
8	5	Eighty-five

T	O	
8	6	Eighty-six

T	O	
8	7	Eighty-seven

T	O	
8	8	Eighty-eight

T	O	
8	9	Eighty-nine

T	O	
9	0	Ninety

NUMBERS FROM 91 TO 100

T	O
9	1

Ninety-one

T	O
9	2

Ninety-two

T	O
9	3

Ninety-three

T	O
9	4

Ninety-four

T	O
9	5

Ninety-five

T	O
9	6

Ninety-six

T	O
9	7

Ninety-seven

T	O
9	8

Ninety-eight

T	O
9	9

Ninety-nine

H	T	O
1	0	0

Hundred

Hundred (100) is a three-digit number.

DO YOU KNOW?
Century is referred to as a period of 100 years.
Also, if you score 100 runs in the game of cricket, it is called a century.

84

A number chart showing numbers from 1 to 100 is given below.

1	2	3	4	5	6	7	8	9	10
11	12	13	14	15	16	17	18	19	20
21	22	23	24	25	26	27	28	29	30
31	32	33	34	35	36	37	38	39	40
41	42	43	44	45	46	47	48	49	50
51	52	53	54	55	56	57	58	59	60
61	62	63	64	65	66	67	68	69	70
71	72	73	74	75	76	77	78	79	80
81	82	83	84	85	86	87	88	89	90
91	92	93	94	95	96	97	98	99	100

MENTAL MATHS

A. What number comes just after 99? _100_

B. Is 25 less than 50? Yes/No

C. Write the missing number in the given sequence.

45 46 ~~47~~ 48 49

EXERCISE 6B

1. Write the missing numbers and read them aloud.

2. Write the number names for the following numbers and read them aloud.

   a. 23 = _Twenty three_

   b. 38 = _thirty eight_

   c. 42 = _forty two_

   d. 78 = _seventy eight_

   e. 94 = _Ninety four_

PLACE VALUE

When we have a 2-digit number, each digit of the number has its own place value.

T	O
2	9

T	O
8	5

The place value of 2 is 20.

The place value of 9 is 9.

The place value of 8 is 80.

The place value of 5 is 5.

EXPANDED FORM

Expanded form of 32

$32 = 30 + 2$

$32 = 3$ tens and 2 ones

T	O
3	2

6   7

Expanded form of 24

$24 = 20 + 4$

$24 = 2$ tens and 4 ones

T	O
2	4

8   3

BEFORE, AFTER AND BETWEEN

5 comes just before 6.

7 comes just after 6.

6 comes between 5 and 7.

55 comes just before 56.

57 comes just after 56.

56 comes between 55 and 57.

1. Write the place value of both the digits in the following numbers.

   a. 74   Place value of 7 is __70__.   b. 61   Place value of 6 is __60__.
            Place value of 4 is __4__.   Place value of 1 is __1__.

2. Write the expanded form of the following numbers.

   a. 54 = __50__ + __4__   b. 67 = __60__ + __7__   c. 83 = __80__ + __3__

3. Write the number that comes just before.

   a. __44__ 45   b. __92__ 93   c. __86__ 87

4. Write the number that comes just after.

   a. 67 __68__   b. 83 __84__   c. 94 __95__

5. Write the number that comes between the given numbers.

   a. 78 __79__ 80   b. 59 __60__ 61   c. 91 __92__ 93

COMPARING NUMBERS

Different Number of Digits

A 2-digit number is always greater than a 1-digit number.

Look at the arrangement given below.

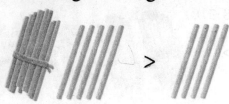

Therefore, 15 > 4.

Same Number of Digits

A number with greater digit in the tens place is greater.

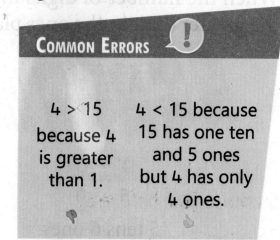

COMMON ERRORS

4 > 15 because 4 is greater than 1.   4 < 15 because 15 has one ten and 5 ones but 4 has only 4 ones.

87

Look at the arrangement given below.

T	O
3	5

3 tens

>

T	O
2	4

2 tens

There is 3 in the tens place.   There is 2 in the tens place.

3 tens is greater than 2 tens. Therefore, 35 > 24.

NOTE

Remember Crego, the crocodile, while comparing numbers.

He loves eating the greater number. He does not eat anything when both the numbers are the same.

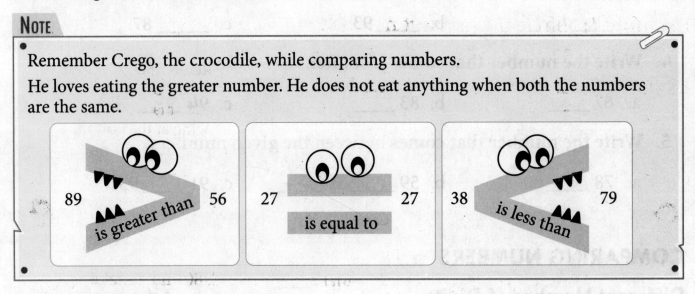

Same Digits in the Tens Place

When the number of digits in the tens place are same, the number with the greater digit in the ones place is greater.

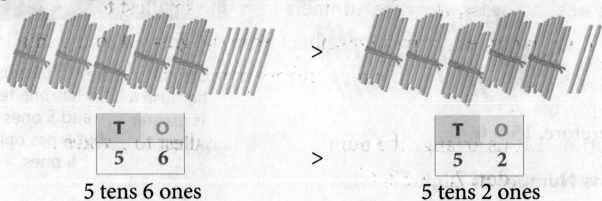

T	O
5	6

5 tens 6 ones

>

T	O
5	2

5 tens 2 ones

There is 6 in the ones place.   There is 2 in the ones place.

6 ones is greater than 2 ones. Therefore, 56 > 52.

Write <, > or =

1. 45 _____ > _____ 23
2. 56 _____ < _____ 78
3. 67 _____ > _____ 21
4. 81 _____ < _____ 89
5. 56 _____ = _____ 56
6. 97 _____ > _____ 73

GREATEST AND SMALLEST

Example 1: Circle the greatest number.

32, 2, (78), 15, 64

Example 2: Circle the smallest number.

54, (19), 73, 22, 69

Go Easy!

Remember: Greatest means being at the top and smallest means being at the bottom

MENTAL MATHS

Fill in the blanks.
A. 60 and 7 make _67_.   B. 7 and 70 make _77_.   C. 80 and 2 make _82_.

INCREASING ORDER AND DECREASING ORDER

In increasing order, we write numbers from the smallest to the greatest.

In decreasing order, we write numbers from the greatest to the smallest.

Example 3: Write the following numbers in increasing order.

82, 15, 49, 32, 7

Solution: Let us arrange the numbers from smallest to greatest.

Increasing order: 7, 15, 32, 49, 82

Example 4: Write the following numbers in decreasing order.
18, 92, 47, 76 and 45.

Solution: Let us arrange the numbers from greatest to smallest.

Decreasing order: 92, 76, 47, 45, 18

PUZZLE!

The secret number is greater than 70. It is less than 85.
Which of the following is the secret number?

56, (78), 98, 65

EXERCISE 6E

1. **Circle the greatest number in the given set of numbers.**

   53, 29, (89), 7, 14

2. **Circle the smallest number in the given set of numbers.**

   35, 91, 42, 29, (8)

3. **Write the following numbers in increasing order.**

   a.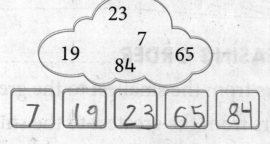

   b.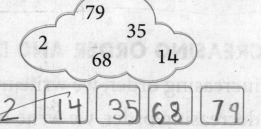

   | 7 | 19 | 23 | 65 | 84 |

   | 2 | 14 | 35 | 68 | 79 |

4. **Write the following numbers in decreasing order.**

   a.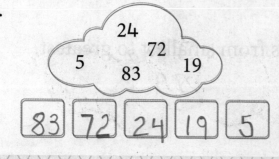

   b.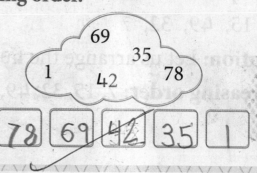

   | 83 | 72 | 24 | 19 | 5 |

   | 78 | 69 | 42 | 35 | 1 |

SKIP COUNTING

When we count forward by a number other than 1, we skip count.
Gary, the grasshopper, skips a number while hopping.

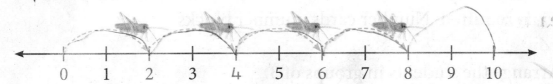

Count in 2s and colour the correct number box to complete the pattern.
A few has been done for you.

1	2	3	4	5	6	7	8	9	10
11	12	13	14	15	16	17	18	19	20
21	22	23	24	25	26	27	28	29	30

Complete the pattern.

2 4 6 8 10 12 14 16 18 20

Count in 5s and colour the correct number box to complete the pattern.

1	2	3	4	5	6	7	8	9	10
11	12	13	14	15	16	17	18	19	20
21	22	23	24	25	26	27	28	29	30
31	32	33	34	35	36	37	38	39	40
41	42	43	44	45	46	47	48	49	50

Complete the pattern.

5 10 15 20 25 30 35 40 45 50

Maths Lab Activity

Aim: To reinforce the concept of grouping in tens (place value) and expanded form of the numbers

Materials required: Number cards, number blocks

Procedure:

1. Arrange the students in groups of 3.
2. Student 1 of the first group picks a number from the number cards, say 27.
3. Student 2 uses the number blocks to represent the number.
4. Student 3 expresses the number in its expanded form in his/her notebook.
5. The activity is repeated for five times with different numbers.
6. Students can then compare the five numbers and tell which number is the smallest and which number is the greatest.
7. Repeat the activity till every student of each group gets a chance.

CONCEPT MAP

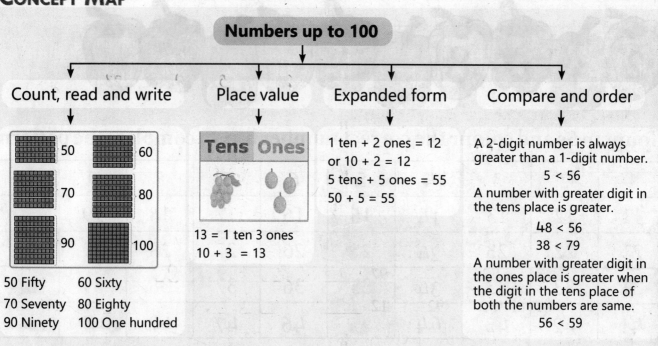

Numbers up to 100

Count, read and write

50	60
70	80
90	100

50 Fifty 60 Sixty
70 Seventy 80 Eighty
90 Ninety 100 One hundred

Place value

Tens Ones

13 = 1 ten 3 ones
10 + 3 = 13

Expanded form

1 ten + 2 ones = 12
or 10 + 2 = 12
5 tens + 5 ones = 55
50 + 5 = 55

Compare and order

A 2-digit number is always greater than a 1-digit number.
5 < 56
A number with greater digit in the tens place is greater.
48 < 56
38 < 79
A number with greater digit in the ones place is greater when the digit in the tens place of both the numbers are same.
56 < 59

KEY CONCEPTS

- A number with greater digit in the tens place is greater.
- When the digits in the tens place are same, we compare the ones digits. The number with greater digit at the ones place is greater.
- The number 100 (hundred) is a 3-digit number.

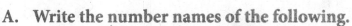

A. Write the number names of the following.

1. 23 _Twenty three_   2. 39 _Thirty nine_

3. 47 _Forty seven_   4. 56 _Fifty six_

B. Fill in the blanks.

1. 4 tens + 3 ones = _43_   2. 7 tens + 6 ones = _76_

3. 9 tens + 2 ones = _92_   4. 50 + 8 = _58_

5. 70 + 1 = _71_   6. 5 tens + 8 ones = _58_

C. Fill in the numbers that come in between the given numbers.

1. 31 _32_ 33

2. 46 _47_, _48_, _49_ 50

3. 71 _72_, _73_, _74_ 75

4. 92 _93_, _94_, _95_ 96

D. Tick (✓) the greatest number and cross (✗) the smallest number.

1. 35   48   15   90✓ ✗   2. 70   51   39   82✓   23✗

E. Circle all the numbers smaller than 72.

(52)   (28)   80   91   (34)

F. Circle all the numbers greater than 61.

(92)   (71)   54   (88)   29

G. Write the given numbers in increasing order.

1. 23   8   52   12   97   _8, 12, 23, 52, 97_

2. 85   21   67   92   12   _12, 21, 67, 85, 92_

H. Write the given numbers in decreasing order.

1. 26   58   71   69   21   _71, 69, 58, 26, 21_

2. 52   78   43   8   12   _78, 52, 43, 12, 8_

I. Complete the pattern.

1. 10,   20,   30,   40, _50, 60, 70, 80_

2. 3,   6,   9,   12, _15, 18, 21, 24_

Proof 30|9

SKILL UP!

A. 21 CS | Creativity and innovation | AI | EL

Make your own hundred chart. Colour the numbers according to the place value of the digits. Give red colour to the numbers that have 7 in the ones place. Observe the pattern and write in your notebook. Make some more such patterns.

B. 21 CS | Critical thinking, Life skills | EL | CC | Integration with Environmental Studies

Amit's father said that it is very important to grow trees to save the environment. So, he planted 80 mango trees, 45 guava trees, 73 apple trees, 29 bananas trees and 62 lemon trees in his orchard. Write down the names of these trees according to the decreasing order of their quantity.

C. 21 CS | Critical thinking, Information literacy

I am greater than 84. I am less than 87. I am 4 more than 82. What number am I?

| 85 | 86 | 87 | 88 |

SUSTAINABLE DEVELOPMENT **GOALS**

Question B is related to SDG 13 Climate Action and SDG 15 Life on Land. Do you plant trees? Find out how do trees save the environment.

WORKSHEET 6

HW

21 CS · Critical thinking, Information literacy

Can you help the pirate reach the treasure? Answer the questions in sequence from a to j and colour the boxes to make the path.

a. 0 tens + 1 one = 1
b. Number just before 13 12
c. 2 tens + 3 ones = 23
d. Number between 33 and 35 34
e. Forty-five = 45
f. Smallest number among 89, 56, 67 56
g. 6 tens and 7 ones = 67
h. Number before 79 78
i. Eighty-nine = 89
j. Another name for century 100

1	11	21	31	41	51	61	71	81	91
2	12	22	32	42	52	62	72	82	92
3	13	23	33	43	53	63	73	83	93
4	14	24	34	44	54	64	74	84	94
5	15	25	35	45	55	65	75	85	95
6	16	26	36	46	56	66	76	86	96
7	17	27	37	47	57	67	77	87	97
8	18	28	38	48	58	68	78	88	98
9	19	29	39	49	59	69	79	89	99
10	20	30	40	50	60	70	80	90	100

HW

1. Which number is the smallest double-digit number?

   a. 10   b. 11   c. 12   d. 13

2. In numbers from 1 to 10, if 1 is the smallest number, then _____ is the greatest number.

   a. 7   b. 8   c. 9   d. 10

3. If there are 17 children at a birthday party, how many cake pieces will be enough?

   a. 11 + 4   b. 12 + 5   c. 9 + 1   d. 13 + 3

4. If there are 39 – 15 seats in a bus, how many people can travel in the bus?

   a. 24   b. 27   c. 29   d. 30

5. Which of the following is not greater than 56?

   a. 67   b. 85   c. 45   d. 94

6. Which of the following shapes will both roll and slide?

   a.   b.

   c.   d.

LEARNING OBJECTIVES

- To add 1-digit and 2-digit numbers up to 99
- To add two or three 2-digit numbers
- To solve word problems

LET'S GET STARTED

Count the number of ants on the anthills in each row and write the answer in the empty anthill.

ADDING TENS

Let us add 4 tens and 1 ten, that is 40 and 10.

This can be explained using a place value chart as given below.

Step 1: Add the ones first.

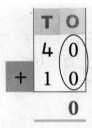

0 ones + 0 ones = 0 ones

Step 2: Add the tens.

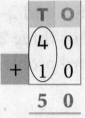

4 tens + 1 ten = 5 tens,
that is 40 + 10 = 50

So, $\boxed{40 + 10 = \textbf{50}}$

Similarly,

$\boxed{20 + 70 = \textbf{90}}$ 1234 $\boxed{10 + 60 = \textbf{70}}$

NOTE

Whenever we add 10 to a number, the ones digit remains the same and the tens digit increases by 1.

8|8|22 Q-W   **EXERCISE 7A**

Add the following numbers and fill in the blanks.

1. 20 + 30 = 50

2. 50 + 10 = 60

3. 40 + 30 = 70

4. 60 + 20 = 80

5. 70 + 20 = 90

6. 80 + 10 = 90

7. 40 + 50 = 90

8. 20 + 40 = 60

9. 50 + 10 = 60

ADDITION OF 2-DIGIT AND 1-DIGIT NUMBERS

Example 1: Find 62 + 5.

Solution:

Adding ones

T	O
6	②
+ 0	⑤
	7

Adding tens

T	O
⑥	2
+ ⓪	5
6	7

62 + 5 using number blocks

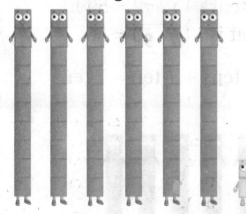 + =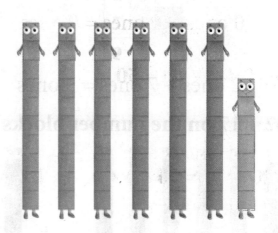

Therefore, 62 + 5 = 67.

8|8|22   H-W   **EXERCISE 7B**

Add the following numbers.

1.
T	O
2	4
+	1
2	5

2.
T	O
7	2
+	3
7	5

3.
T	O
5	6
+	2
5	8

4.
T	O
4	9
+	0
4	9

5.
T	O
8	5
+	4
8	9

6.
T	O
9	3
+	5
9	8

practice it

ADDITION OF TWO 2-DIGIT NUMBERS

To add two 2-digit numbers, first write the numbers in their correct places on the place value chart. Then add the ones digits followed by adding the tens digits.

Example 2: Solve 62 + 17

Solution:

Step 1: Add the ones first.

T	O
6	2
+ 1	7
	9

2 ones + 7 ones = 9 ones

Step 2: Add the tens.

T	O
6	2
+ 1	7
7	9

6 tens + 1 ten = 7 tens

62 + 17 on the number blocks

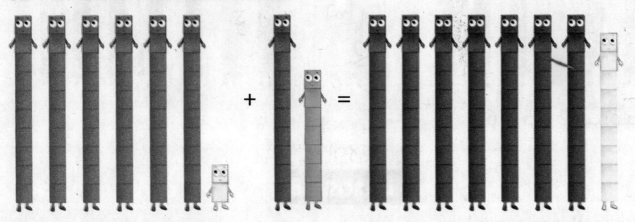

Therefore, 62 + 17 = 79.

MENTAL MATHS

45 + 30 = 75

55 + 4 = 59

12 + 15 = 27

40 + 20 = 60

PUZZLE!

Each number is the total of the two numbers below it. Complete the tree.

ADDITION OF THREE 2-DIGIT NUMBERS

Here also, first add the ones digits followed by adding the tens digits.

Example 3: 12 + 23 + 14

Solution:

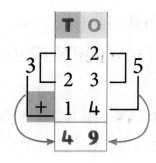

In each column, add the first two digits.

Then, add the sum to the remaining digits.

12 + 23 + 14 on the number blocks

Therefore, 12 + 23 + 14 = 49.

Add the following numbers.

1.

T	O
2	3
+ 1	4
3	7

2.

T	O
7	4
+ 2	5
9	9

3.

T	O
6	1
+ 2	0
8	1

4.

T	O
1	2
3	4
+ 5	1
9	7

5.

T	O
2	3
4	0
+ 1	5
7	8

6.

T	O
6	4
1	2
+ 2	3
9	9

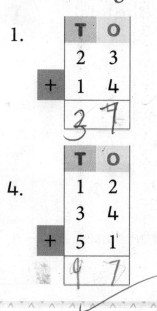

101

WORD PROBLEMS ON ADDITION

Example 4: Emma has 10 stickers. Karan has 12 stickers. Harpreet has 35 stickers. How many stickers do they have altogether?

T	O
1	0
1	2
+ 3	5
5	7

Solution: The number of stickers with Emma = 10

The number of stickers with Karan = 12

The number of stickers with Harpreet = 35

Total number of stickers = 10 + 12 + 35 = 57

So, they have 57 stickers altogether.

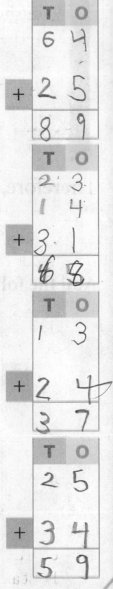

EXERCISE 7D

1. A mango tree has 64 mangoes. An apple tree has 25 apples. How many mangoes and apples are there altogether?

   Solution: There are ___8 9___ mangoes and apples.

T	O
6	4
+ 2	5
8	9

2. Kavya bought 23 oranges and 14 pears. She later bought 31 apples. How many fruits did she buy in all?

   Solution: Kavya bought ___(4 5) 68___ fruits.

T	O
2	3
1	4
+ 3	1
6	8

3. In a pond, there were 13 frogs and 24 ducks. What is the total number of animals in the pond?

   Solution: There are ___3 7___ animals in the pond.

T	O
1	3
+ 2	4
3	7

4. There are 25 sandwiches on one plate. There are 34 sandwiches on another plate. How many sandwiches are there on both the plates?

   Solution: There are ___5 9___ sandwiches on both the plates.

T	O
2	5
+ 3	4
5	9

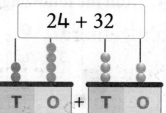

Aim: Developing the concept of addition using spike abacus

Materials required: Two sets of spike abacus, number cards

Procedure:

1. Arrange the students into groups of 4.
2. Student 1 of the first group picks a number card, say 24.
3. Student 2 represents the number on the spike abacus. He/she puts 2 beads in the tens rod and 4 beads in the ones rod.
4. Student 3 picks another number card, say 32.
5. Student 4 represents the number on another set of abacus. He/she puts 3 beads in the tens rod and 2 beads in the ones rod.
6. Student 5 combines the beads of ones and tens rods, respectively. He/she gets 6 beads in the ones rod and 5 beads in the tens rod.
7. All the students write the answer in their notebooks.
8. The activity is repeated till each member of each group gets a turn to add the numbers.

Concept Map

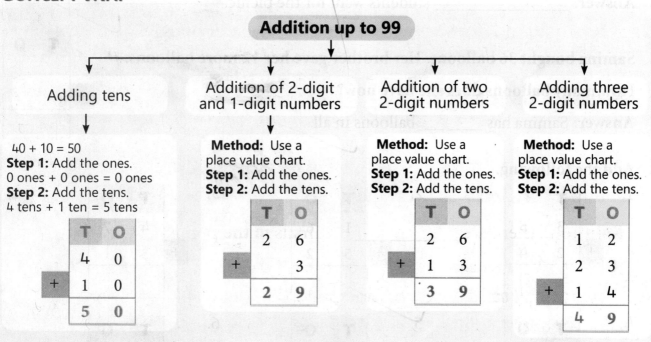

Addition up to 99

Adding tens

$40 + 10 = 50$
Step 1: Add the ones.
0 ones + 0 ones = 0 ones
Step 2: Add the tens.
4 tens + 1 ten = 5 tens

T	O
4	0
+ 1	0
5	0

Addition of 2-digit and 1-digit numbers

Method: Use a place value chart.
Step 1: Add the ones.
Step 2: Add the tens.

T	O
2	6
+	3
2	9

Addition of two 2-digit numbers

Method: Use a place value chart.
Step 1: Add the ones.
Step 2: Add the tens.

T	O
2	6
+ 1	3
3	9

Adding three 2-digit numbers

Method: Use a place value chart.
Step 1: Add the ones.
Step 2: Add the tens.

T	O
1	2
2	3
+ 1	4
4	9

Key Concepts

- While adding, place the digits according to their place value in a place value chart.
- First add the digits in the ones column and then add the digits in the tens column.

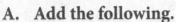
H-W

A. Add the following.

1.

T	O
3	4
+	1
3	8

2.

T	O
7	9
2	0
9	9

3.

T	O
2	5
+ 7	1
9	6

4.

T	O
1	2
3	4
+ 2	1
6	7

5.

T	O
3	0
2	1
+ 3	5
9	6

6.

T	O
4	1
4	0
+	8
8	9

B. A class of 24 boys and 35 girls went for a picnic. How many students went for the picnic?

Answer: ___5 9___ students went for the picnic.

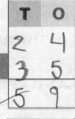

T	O
2	4
+ 3	5
5	9

C. Samina bought 36 balloons. Her brother gave her 12 more balloons. How many balloons does she have now?

Answer: Samina has ___4 8___ balloons in all.

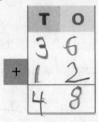

T	O
3	6
+ 1	2
4	8

D. Add the following.

1.

T	O
3	5
+ 2	4
5	9

2.

T	O
1	6
+ 5	2
6	8

3.

T	O
4	7
+ 3	1
7	8

4.

T	O
2	3
+ 5	5
7	8

5.

T	O
6	4
+ 2	3
8	7

6.

T	O
7	2
+ 1	4
8	6

SKILL UP!

A.

Learn addition of numbers by taking the help of the pages of a book.

Add 23 + 11.

Open a book to page 23.

Starting from page 24, count 11 pages. That is, 23 + 11 = 34. So, you will reach page 34. Which topic is given on that page?

Now solve the following with the help of the pages of your book. Mention the topics given on these pages.

a. 67 + 2   b. 45 + 12 + 11   c. 25 + 12

Write a report on your findings.

B. 21 CS / Life Skills   HQ   Cooperation and collaborative living

Ahmad and Sana usually help their mother in washing the utensils. Ahmad washed 12 plates and Sana washed 20 spoons.

How many utensils did they wash in all?

SUSTAINABLE DEVELOPMENT GOALS

Question B is related to SDG 3 Good Health and Well-Being and SDG 5 Gender Equality. Cleaning utensils would help in keeping good health. Ahmad and Sana, who are brother and sister, help their parents without saying that it is a boy's or a girl's work. Do you help your parents?

WORKSHEET 7

H-W

21 CS   Critical thinking

Help the frog to reach its babies at home. The frog starts from the water lily pad with seventy-eight and then hops as per the given clue sums (a to f) to form a path towards home. Solve these sums and colour the water lily pads forming the path.

a.

T	O
3	8
+ 2	1
5	9

b.

T	O
7	5
+ 2	3
9	8

c.

T	O
1	0
+	2
1	2

d.

T	O
3	5
+ 5	0
8	5

e.

T	O
3	3
+ 1	3
4	6

f.

T	O
5	6
+ 3	2
8	8

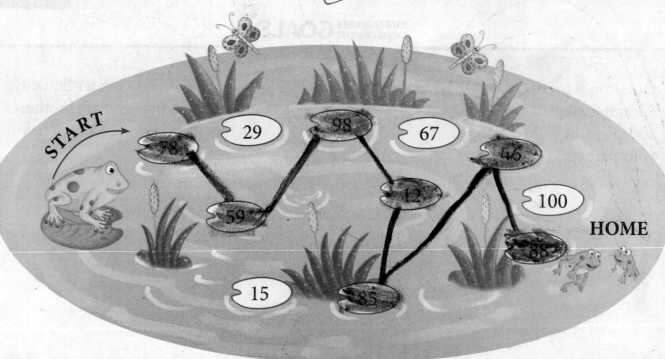

LEARNING OBJECTIVES

- To subtract 1-digit and 2-digit numbers up to 99
- To subtract two 2-digit numbers
- To solve word problems

LET'S GET STARTED

21 CS / Information literacy   AI

Subtract the numbers and colour accordingly.

$$10 - 9 = \bullet$$

$$10 - 5 = \bullet$$

$$9 - 0 = \bullet$$

$$7 - 1 = \bullet$$

$$19 - 11 = \bullet$$

$$17 - 14 = \bullet$$

$$15 - 11 = \bullet$$

$$17 - 10 = \bullet$$

$$5 - 3 = \bullet$$

SUBTRACTING TENS

Let us subtract 4 tens and 3 tens.

This can be explained by a place value chart.

Step 1: Subtract the ones first.

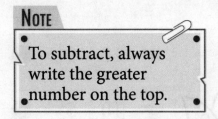

Step 2: Subtract the tens.

	T	O
	4	0
−	3	0
	1	0

0 ones − 0 ones = 0 ones

4 tens − 3 tens = 1 ten

40 − 30 = 10

NOTE

To subtract, always write the greater number on the top.

Whenever we subtract 10 from a number, the ones digit remains the same and the tens digit reduces by 1.

COMMON ERRORS

	T	O
	6	7
−	1	0
	5	0

	T	O
	6	7
−	1	0
	5	7

EXERCISE 8A

1. Subtract the following.

   a. 50 − 10 = 40   b. 80 − 30 = 50   c. 90 − 10 = 80   d. 70 − 20 = 50

   e. 30 − 10 = 20   f. 60 − 10 = 50   g. 40 − 30 = 10   h. 50 − 20 = 30

2. Subtract the following.

   a. 77 − 10 = 67   b. 57 − 10 = 47   c. 93 − 10 = 83   d. 89 − 10 = 79

SUBTRACTING 1-DIGIT NUMBER FROM 2-DIGIT NUMBER

Example 1: Subtract 7 from 59.

Solution: First, subtract the digits in the ones column. Then subtract the digits in the tens column. As 7 is a 1-digit number, it has 0 tens. So, there is nothing to be subtracted from 5 tens. Write 5 as it is in the tens column.

Go Easy!

How can you check your answer?

Add the answer to the smaller number to get the greater number.

T	O
5	2
+	7
5	9

59 – 7 on number blocks

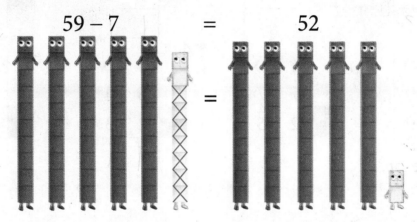

So, 59 – 7 = 52.

SUBTRACTION OF TWO 2-DIGIT NUMBERS

To subtract two 2-digit numbers, first write the numbers in their correct places on the place value chart. Then subtract the ones digits followed by subtracting the tens digits.

Example 2: Solve 58 – 27.

Solution: Step 1: Subtract the ones first.

T	O
5	8
– 2	7
	1

8 ones – 7 ones = 1 one

Step 2: Subtract the tens.

T	O
5	8
– 2	7
3	1

5 tens – 2 tens = 3 tens

Therefore, 58 – 27 = 31.

Subtract the following.

1.
T	O
2	4
−	3
2	1

2.
T	O
5	9
− 2	4
3	5

3.
T	O
6	8
−	5
6	3

4.
T	O
7	3
− 6	1
1	2

5.
T	O
9	8
− 2	6
7	2

6.
T	O
4	6
−	5
4	1

7.
T	O
2	4
− 1	3
1	1

8.
T	O
5	9
− 2	0
3	9

9.
T	O
8	0
− 6	0
2	0

10.
T	O
7	7
− 2	5
5	2

11.
T	O
6	4
− 2	3
4	1

12.
T	O
5	9
− 3	4
2	5

MENTAL MATHS

Solve and then match the subtraction problem to its corresponding addition check. One has been done for you.

$14 - 3 = 11$ $10 + 8 = 18$

$18 - 8 = 10$ $11 + 6 = 17$

$15 - 4 = 11$ $12 + 4 = 16$

$17 - 6 = 11$ $11 + 4 = 15$

$16 - 4 = 12$ $11 + 3 = 14$

WORD PROBLEMS ON SUBTRACTION

Example 3: There are 35 children in a birthday party. Eleven children went back home after a while. How many children are still present at the birthday party?

Solution: The number of children at the birthday party = 35

The number of children that went home = 11

The number of children that are still at the birthday party = 35 − 11 = 24

T	O
3	5
− 1	1
2	**4**

24 children are still present at the birthday party.

EXERCISE 8C

1. **Iqbal has 45 flowers. 21 flowers are blue. The rest are red. How many flowers are red?**

   Solution: ___2 4___ flowers are red.

T	O
4	5
− 2	1
2	4

2. **Ajay had 56 marbles. He lost 14 marbles out of them. How many marbles were left with him?**

   Solution: Ajay is left with ___4 2___ marbles.

T	O
5	6
− 1	4
4	2

3. **Arvind baked 39 cakes in one day. He sold 8 cakes out of them. How many cakes were left with him?**

   Solution: ___3 1___ cakes were left with him.

T	O
3	9
− 3	8
3	1

4. **There are 58 apples. 26 are rotten. How many apples are in good condition?**

   Solution: ___3 1___ apples are in good condition.

T	O
5	8
− 2	6
3	1

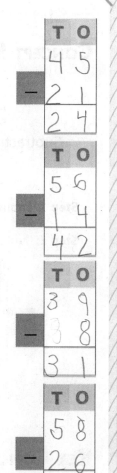

Aim: To reinforce subtraction skills using a number grid

Materials required: Number grid 1 to 99, number cards numbered from 0 to 99 and beads

Procedure:

1	2	3	4	5	6	7	8	9	10
11	12	13	14	15	16	17	18	19	20
21	22	23	24	25	26	27	28	29	30
31	32	33	34	35	36	37	38	39	40
41	42	43	44	45	46	47	48	49	50
51	52	53	54	55	56	57	58	59	60
61	62	63	64	65	66	67	68	69	70
71	72	73	74	75	76	77	78	79	80
81	82	83	84	85	86	87	88	89	90
91	92	93	94	95	96	97	98	99	

1. Arrange the class into groups of 5.
2. Student 1 of first group takes out a number card from the bowl, say 37.
3. Student 2 puts beads from 1 to 37 on the number grid.
4. Student 3 takes out another number card from the bowl, say 23.
5. Student 4 removes 23 beads.
6. Student 5 counts the number of beads left on the number grid.
7. Continue the activity till each member of each group gets a turn to subtract numbers.

CONCEPT MAP

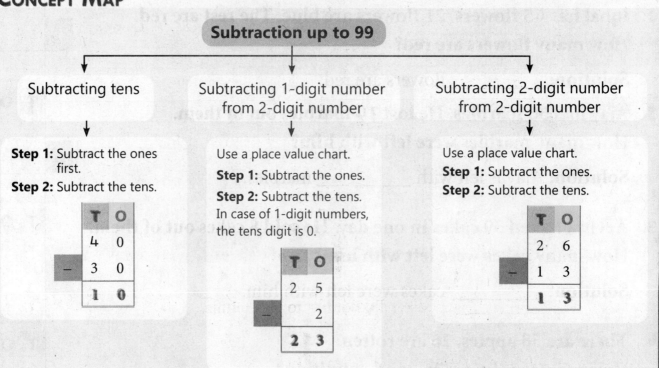

Subtraction up to 99

Subtracting tens

Step 1: Subtract the ones first.
Step 2: Subtract the tens.

T	O
4	0
− 3	0
1	0

Subtracting 1-digit number from 2-digit number

Use a place value chart.
Step 1: Subtract the ones.
Step 2: Subtract the tens.
In case of 1-digit numbers, the tens digit is 0.

T	O
2	5
−	2
2	3

Subtracting 2-digit number from 2-digit number

Use a place value chart.
Step 1: Subtract the ones.
Step 2: Subtract the tens.

T	O
2	6
− 1	3
1	3

KEY CONCEPTS

Whenever we subtract 10 from a number, the ones digit remains the same and the tens digit reduces by 1.

A. Circle the correct answer.

1. $40 - 30 =$ 〔 10 〕

   10   20   30   40

2. $90 - 10 =$ 〔 80 〕

   60   70   80   90

B. Match the questions in row A to their answers in row B.

Row A

1.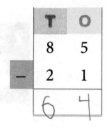

T	O
8	5
− 2	1
6	4

2.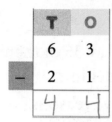

T	O
6	3
− 2	1
4	4

3.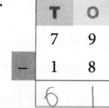

T	O
7	9
− 1	8
6	1

4.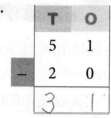

T	O
5	1
− 2	0
3	1

Row B

a. 61   b. 64   c. 42   d. 31

C. Subtract the following.

1.
T	O
8	7
− 4	5

2.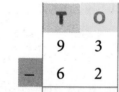
T	O
9	3
− 6	2

3.
T	O
4	8
− 2	3

4.
T	O
6	6
− 3	3

5.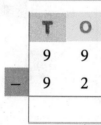
T	O
9	9
− 9	2

6.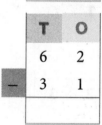
T	O
6	2
− 3	1

D. Out of 49 children in a sports club, 23 liked to play tennis. How many children did not like to play tennis?

Solution: _____ children did not like to play tennis.

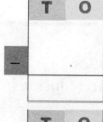

E. The teacher bought 56 chocolates. She distributed 42 chocolates among the students. How many chocolates were left with her?

Solution: _____ chocolates were left with her.

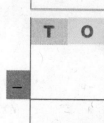

A.

Play this game in pairs. Each child starts with a score of 99. Throw a dice and subtract the number on the dice from your score.
The one whose score becomes less than 10 first, wins the game.

B.

Ishan has 55 loaves of bread. He gave away 35 of them to the needy. How many loaves are left with him?
Do you think he did the right thing? Give reasons.

C.

Fill in the boxes.

T	O
7	☐
−	3
7	2

To find what number will come in the blank, add 3 and 2.
3 + 2 = 5

T	O
7	5
−	3
7	2

Solve the following using the method given above.

T	O
2	☐
−	3
2	3

T	O
6	☐
−	8
6	1

T	O
5	☐
−	2
5	5

T	O
4	☐
−	5
4	0

SUSTAINABLE DEVELOPMENT GOALS

Question B is related to SDG 2 Zero Hunger. Sharing your food with the needy would help in reducing hunger, even in a small way.

All living beings are an important part of nature. They need water and food to survive on land. Bees get honey from flowers.

Which path should the bee take to find the flower for honey? Solve each problem to find the path. Draw a line and then connect each number that has 4 in the tens place to find the path.

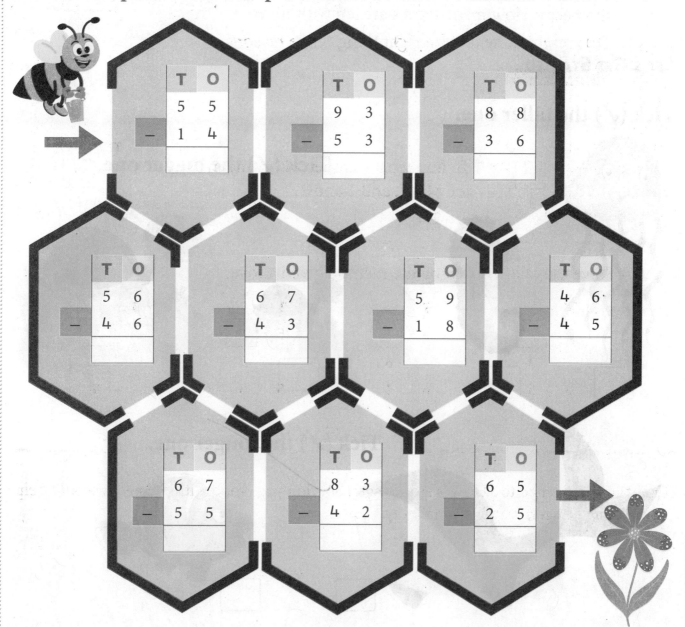

9 Measurement

- To measure length using non-standard units
- To measure mass using non-standard units
- To compare heavier and lighter objects
- To measure and compare capacity using containers

LET'S GET STARTED

Tick (✓) the taller one.

Tick (✓) the bigger one.

Tick (✓) the longer one.

LENGTH

Using Body Parts to Measure Length

We can measure the length of the objects with the help of our hand span, foot span, foot pace or cubit (arm length).

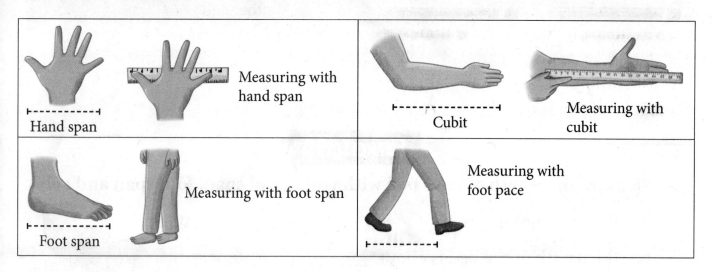

Measuring with hand span

Hand span

Cubit

Measuring with cubit

Measuring with foot span

Foot span

Measuring with foot pace

How tall are the following objects? Let us find the height of these objects by counting the paper pins.

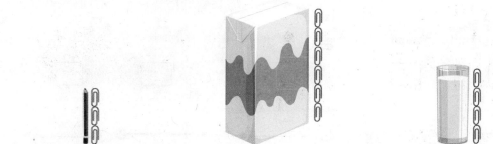

The pencil is as tall as 3 pins.

The milk carton is as tall as 6 pins.

The milk glass is as tall as 4 pins.

Therefore, the milk carton is the tallest and the pencil is the shortest.

CROSSWORD

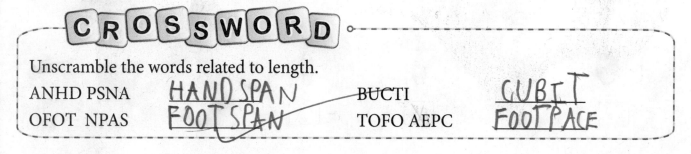

Unscramble the words related to length.

ANHD PSNA — HANDSPAN

OFOT NPAS — FOOTSPAN

BUCTI — CUBIT

TOFO AEPC — FOOTPACE

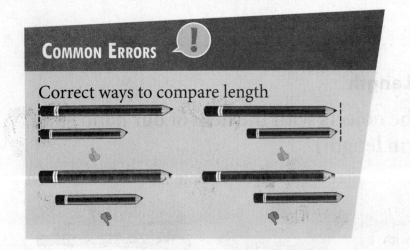

Correct ways to compare length

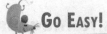 **Go Easy!**

To measure the length of an object, we must start from the one end and finish at the other end.

EXERCISE 9A

1. Measure the length of your bed with your hand span, foot span and cubit.

   a. The length of the bed is about _____14_____ hand spans.

   b. The length of the bed is about _____13_____ foot spans.

   c. The length of the bed is about _____7_____ cubit.

2. Tick (✔) the longest.

   a.
   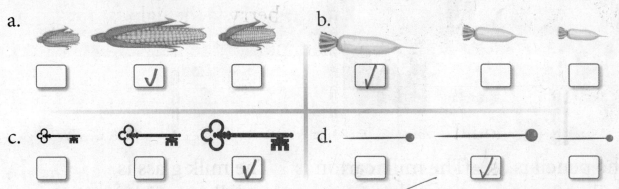
   ☐ ✓ ☐

   b.
   ✓ ☐ ☐

   c. ☐ ☐ ✓

   d. ☐ ✓ ☐

3. Tick (✔) the tallest and cross (✗) the shortest.

   a.
   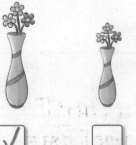

   ✓ ☐ ✗

   b.

   ✗ ☐ ✓

MASS

Look at the children playing on the seesaw.

Just like the seesaw, while using a simple balance, the heavier object drops towards the ground, whereas the lighter object lifts upwards.

Comparing More Than Two Objects

Pineapple is lighter than pumpkin.
Pineapple is heavier than strawberry.
Strawberry is the lightest.
Pumpkin is the heaviest.

CAPACITY

The amount of liquid that a container can hold is called its **capacity**.

Let us have a look at these glasses.

Glasses A and B can hold the same amount of juice. Glass C holds lesser amount of juice. Therefore, glasses A and B have the same capacity. Glass C has lesser capacity than glasses A and B.

Comparing Capacity

We can use containers to compare capacities.

All the milk from Bottle A and Bottle B is poured into glasses. These glasses are of the same size.

Bottle A

Bottle B

Do you know?
The amount of liquid does not change when it is poured into a different container, unless the liquid is spilled over.

Capacity of Bottle A = Total capacity of 3 glasses of milk

Capacity of Bottle B = Total capacity of 5 glasses of milk
Therefore, Bottle B has more capacity than Bottle A.

EXERCISE 9B

1. Write H for the heavier object and L for the lighter object in the space provided.

a.   b.

H   L   L   H

2. Tick (✔) the heaviest.

3. Tick (✔) the container that has a greater capacity.

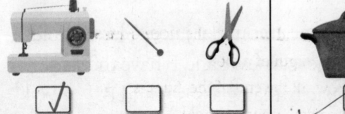

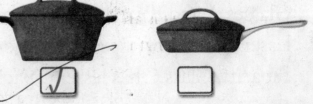

✓   ☐   ☐   ✓   ☐

Aim: To develop the skill of measuring objects using non-standard units

Materials required: Long strings of same length, objects to be measured

Procedure:

1. Make a group of 4 students to demonstrate the activity in the class.
2. Student 1 measures the length of a notebook using a string.
3. Student 2 measures the length of another notebook using a string.
4. Student 3 records the observations as given below.

Objects	Length
Notebook 1	1 complete string and more
Notebook 2	1 complete string

5. Student 4 compares both the objects using the observations and tells which of the two notebooks is the longest.
   Repeat the activity with different objects.

CONCEPT MAP

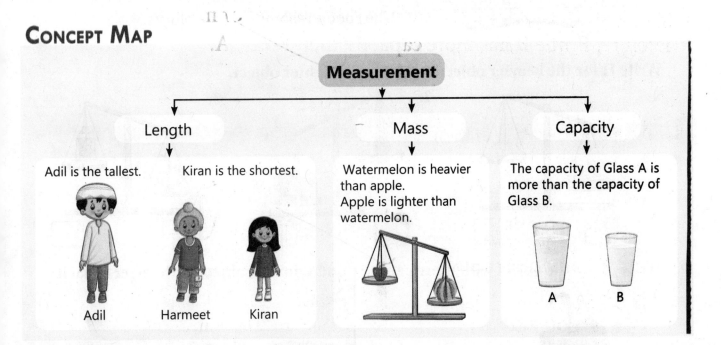

KEY CONCEPTS

- **Hand span:** The distance covered by a hand when all the fingers are stretched
- **Foot span:** The length covered by the length of a foot
- **Cubit:** The length covered from elbow till the end of the fingers
- **Capacity:** The amount of liquid that a container can hold

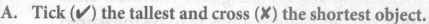

A. Tick (✔) the tallest and cross (✗) the shortest object.

1.

✓ ☐ ✗

2.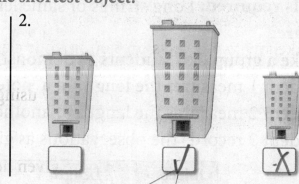

☐ ✓ ✗

B. How long are the given objects?

1.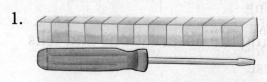

The screwdriver is about ☐12☐ blocks.

2.

The spoon is about ☐10☐ blocks.

C. Write H for the heavier object and L for the lighter object.

1. 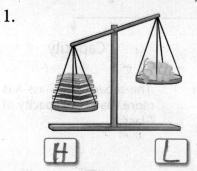 2. 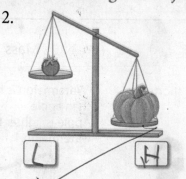 3.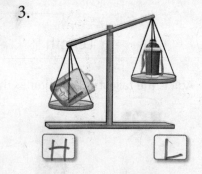

H L   L H   H L

D. Write M for the object with more capacity and L for the object with lesser capacity.

1.

M L

2.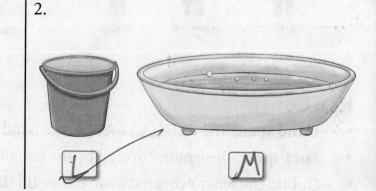

L M

SKILL UP!

A.

Take any two objects present in your classroom, say duster and a small packet of chalks. Which object do you think is longer? Use paper pins to find the answer. Repeat the activity using various objects.

B.

Two glasses of different sizes are given here.

Which glass has a greater capacity?

If we want to drink less water, should we fill the bigger glass and throw the extra water away? Should we fill the smaller glass and drink all the water instead? Do you think we should waste water?

C.

Rahul is taller than Ayaan. Ravi is the tallest.
Write the names of the boys.

Rahul   Ayaan   Ravi

SUSTAINABLE DEVELOPMENT GOALS

Question B is related to SDG 6 Clean Water and Sanitation. Water is very precious. We should not waste it. If we keep wasting water, there would not be any water left for use. Think about your daily routine. Did you waste any water today?

WORKSHEET 9

Read, draw and colour.

Shelf A	• Draw a toy shorter than the teddy. • Draw a toy taller than the teddy.
Shelf B	• Draw a fruit lighter than the apple. • Draw a fruit heavier than the apple.
Shelf C	• Draw a container that can hold less water than the glass. • Draw a container that can hold more water than the glass.

Shelf A

Shelf B

Shelf C

10 Time and Money

LEARNING OBJECTIVES

- To read and show time to the hour in a clock
- To relate time to daily activities
- To know the days of a week
- To learn about coins and notes used in India
- To study different combinations of coins and notes

LET'S GET STARTED

Which activities do you do during the day or night? Fill in the blanks using the following letters. Are there any activities that you do in the morning as well as night?

M = Morning   **A** = Afternoon   **E** = Evening   **N** = Night

Reading Time

A clock tells us exactly what time of the day it is. There are three hands in a clock.

◆── The longer hand is the **minute hand**.

◆── The shorter hand is the **hour hand**.

── The thin and long hand is the second hand.

We see numbers from 1 to 12 on the face of a clock. The minute hand moves faster than the hour hand. The second hand moves faster than the minute hand.

In an hour, the hour hand moves from one number to the next number and the minute hand completes one round on the face of the clock.

In the given clock, the minute hand is at 12.

The hour hand is at 9.

Time is 9 o'clock.

Time is written in two ways: 9 o'clock or 9:00.

In the given clock, both the hands are at 12. Time is 12 o'clock or 12:00.

COMMON ERRORS

It is 7 o'clock. 👎

It is 12 o'clock. 👎

Showing Time

Let us show 10:00 on a clock.

Step 1: Draw the hour hand at 10.

Step 2: Draw the minute hand at 12.

Step 1   **Step 2**

1. **Fill in the blanks.**

a.

Minute hand is at ___12___

Hour hand is at ___5___

Time = ___5 o'clock___ or

___5:00___

b.

Minute hand is at ___12___

Hour hand is at ___7___

Time = ___7 o'clock___ or

___7:00___

c.

Minute hand is at ___12___

Hour hand is at ___1___

Time = ___1 o'clock___ or

___1:00___

2. **Draw the hour hand in each clock to show the given time.**

a.

4 o'clock or 4:00

b.

8 o'clock or 8:00

c.

2 o'clock or 2:00

3. **Draw the hour hand and the minute hand to show the given time.**

a.

1 o'clock or 1:00

b.

5 o'clock or 5:00

c.

9 o'clock or 9:00

WHAT TAKES MORE TIME?

Tick (✓) the activity that will take longer.

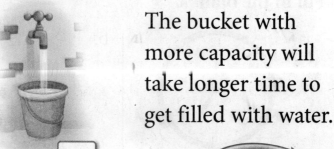

The bucket with more capacity will take longer time to get filled with water.

DAYS OF THE WEEK

There are 7 days in a week.

Monday is the first day of the week.

Sunday is the last day of the week.

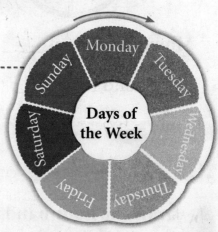

EXERCISE 10B

1. **Have a look at Harleen's chore chart.**

Monday	Tuesday	Wednesday	Thursday	Friday	Saturday	Sunday
Make bed	Water plants	Throw trash	Help mom	Help dad	Clean room	

On which day, Harleen

a. made her bed? _Monday_

b. cleaned her room? _Saturday_

c. watered the plants? _Tuesday_

d. threw the trash? _Wednesday_

2. **Tick (✓) the activity in each row that will take longer time.**

a. Brushing your teeth ☐ Washing the car ✓

b. Eating lunch ✓ Baking a cake ✓

c. Reading a story book ✓ Writing your name ✓

MONEY

John sometimes goes to the market with his mother. His mother gives money to the shopkeeper whenever they buy grocery items.

When you need to buy something, you have to pay money for it.

In India, we count the money in rupees and paise. There are coins and notes of different values.

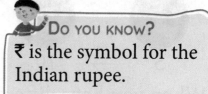

Do you know?
₹ is the symbol for the Indian rupee.

Coins

The value of each coin is written on one side of it.

One-rupee coin, ₹1   Two-rupee coin, ₹2   Five-rupee coin, ₹5   Ten-rupee coin, ₹10

Notes

Given below are the commonly used notes.

1 rupee or ₹1   2 rupees or ₹2   5 rupees or ₹5

10 rupees or ₹10   20 rupees or ₹20

Note
1 rupee, 2 rupees, 5 rupees and 10 rupees are available in notes and coins.

50 rupees or ₹50   100 rupees or ₹100

COMBINATIONS OF COINS AND NOTES

Coins having the same value can be counted or added in the following way.

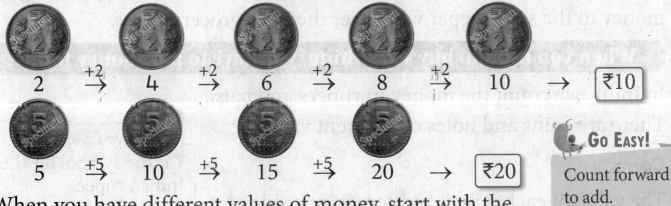

$$2 \xrightarrow{+2} 4 \xrightarrow{+2} 6 \xrightarrow{+2} 8 \xrightarrow{+2} 10 \rightarrow \boxed{₹10}$$

$$5 \xrightarrow{+5} 10 \xrightarrow{+5} 15 \xrightarrow{+5} 20 \rightarrow \boxed{₹20}$$

Go Easy!

Count forward to add.

When you have different values of money, start with the greatest value to count or add.

$$5 \xrightarrow{+2} 7 \xrightarrow{+2} 9 \xrightarrow{+1} 10 \rightarrow \boxed{₹10}$$

$$20 \xrightarrow{+5} 25 \xrightarrow{+2} 27 \xrightarrow{+2} 29 \xrightarrow{+1} 30 \rightarrow \boxed{₹30}$$

EXERCISE 10C

Find the cost of each item and write it on the price tag.

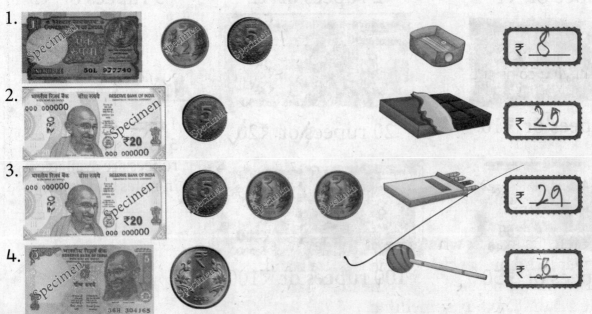

1. ₹ 8
2. ₹ 25
3. ₹ 29
4. ₹ 6

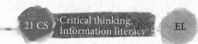
Aim: To understand the importance of time and planning

Materials required: Pencil, a sheet of paper

Procedure:

1. Keep the time interval of one hour. Record the time intervals and the corresponding activities performed on a holiday in a table as shown.

Time intervals of 1 hour	Activity performed
(Morning) 6 o'clock to 7 o'clock	Sleeping
7:00 to 8:00	
8:00 to 9:00	

2. Calculate the time spent in watching TV, studying and playing.
3. Ask your friends to create a similar table. Then discuss with them and make a comparison with their study time and play time.

Concept Map

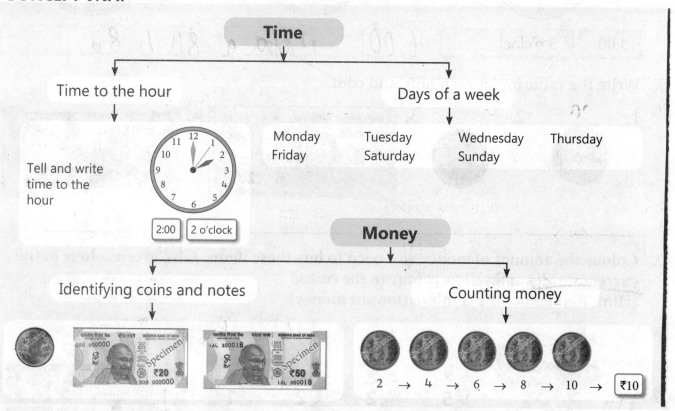

Key Concepts

- A clock tells us exactly what time of the day it is.
- The longer hand on the clock is the minute hand.
- The shorter hand on the clock is the hour hand.
- You need money to buy something.

A. Draw the hands of the clock to show the given time.

1. 1 o'clock
2. 7:00
3. 12 o'clock
4. 9:00

B. Write the time. One has been done for you.

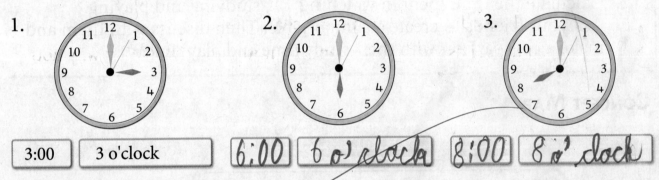

1. 3:00   3 o'clock
2. 6:00   6 o'clock
3. 8:00   8 o'clock

C. Write the value under each note and coin.

1. 2₹
2. 5₹
3. 20₹
4. 50₹

D. Colour the amount of money you need to buy these items. Give green colour to the currency notes and yellow colour to the coins.
(Hint: Remember the combinations of money)

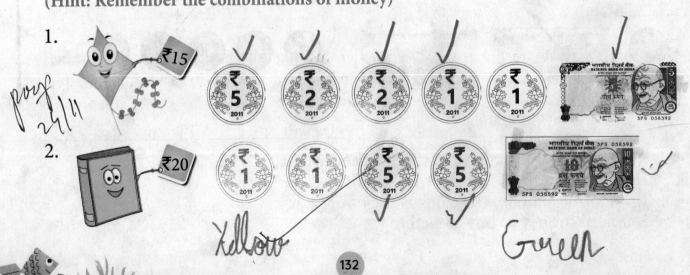

1. ₹15
2. ₹20

Yellow   Green

A. 21 CS — Creativity and innovation, Information literacy — AI

Organize your weekly activities by making a weekly planner. Set up your own colour theme. Use different colours to identify the tasks.

B. 21 CS — Critical thinking, Life Skills

Tanya needs to make a chart and submit it to her teacher on Thursday. She did not make the chart. She submitted the chart on the day next to Thursday.

On which day did Tanya submit the chart?

Do you think it is important to finish our work on time? Why/why not?

C. 21 CS — Critical thinking

Samina has ₹50. She needs to buy three pencil sets.

Circle the pencil sets that she can buy with ₹50. She plans to donate these pencils to an orphanage.

₹20   ₹20   ₹10   ₹20

SUSTAINABLE DEVELOPMENT **GOALS**

Question C is related to SDG 1 No Poverty. Samina might be able to buy three pencil sets. However, there are many who cannot buy even one pencil. What do you think you can do to help those people who cannot buy even one pencil?

21 CS / Critical thinking

A clockmaker makes and repairs clocks.

The picture shows a clockmaker who has repaired a few clocks and has hung them on the wall. Two clocks still need repairing and are lying on the table.

Identify the time in each clock and write it in the given space. ~~What is missing in all the clocks?~~

11 Data Handling

LET'S GET STARTED

Count and write the number of animals and birds.

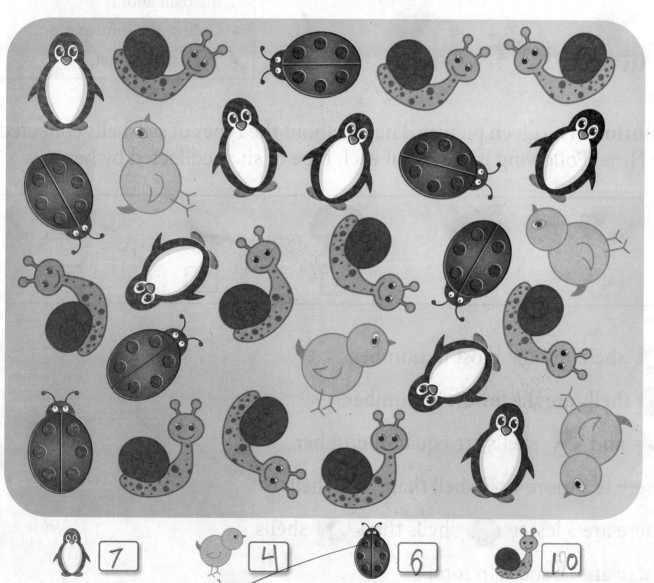

 7   4   6   10

DATA

Data are information that has numbers. We count the number of objects. It helps us to know how many of each object do we have.

Example 1: Hina loves collecting seashells. Following are the types of shells collected by her. How should we understand the given information?

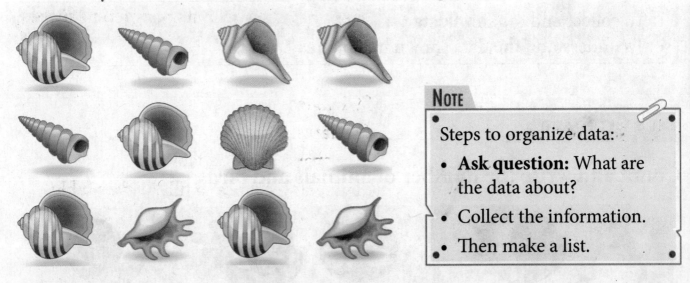

> **NOTE**
>
> Steps to organize data:
> - **Ask question:** What are the data about?
> - Collect the information.
> - Then make a list.

Solution: The given picture data are about the types of seashells collected by Hina. Following is the list of each type of shell collected by her.

| 4 | 3 | 1 | 2 | 2 |

shells are the most in number.

shells are the fewest in number.

and shells are equal in number.

There is 1 more shell than shells.

There are 3 lesser shells than shells.

There are 12 shells in total.

136

Maths Lab Activity

Aim: To collect, record and interpret data

Materials required: Cut-outs of different shapes, namely circles, rectangles, triangles and squares

Procedure:

1. Make a group of 5 students and provide them cut-outs of different shapes.
2. Student 1 counts the number of circles.
3. Student 2 counts the number of rectangles.
4. Student 3 counts the number of triangles.
5. Student 4 counts the number of squares.
6. Student 5 records the count of each shape in a data table.
7. Repeat the activity till every student gets a chance to fill the data table.

Shapes	Circles	Triangles	Rectangles	Squares	Total
How many?					

CONCEPT MAP

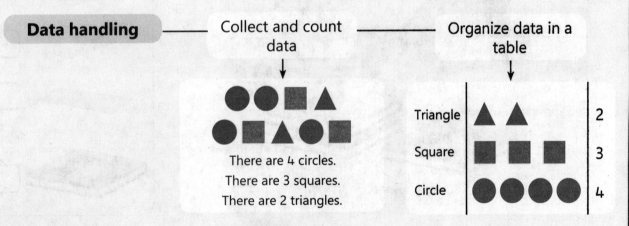

KEY CONCEPTS

- **Data:** Information that has numbers
- We can organize data and interpret data.

CHAPTER REVISION

A. Write the number of items of each kind in the given table.

Fill in the blanks.

1. Which fruit is the most in number? _orange_
2. Which fruit is the least in number? _cherry_
3. How many fruits are there in all? _22_

Fruit					
Number	6	5	4	4	3

B. Count and write the number of each item.

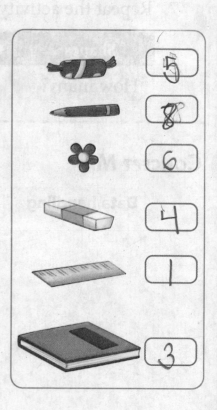

Fill in the blanks.

1. How many items are there in all? _27_
2. How many erasers are there? _4_
3. The toffees are _3_ (2/3) lesser than the pencil colours.
4. The erasers are _less_ (more/less) than the flowers.
5. The _scale_ is the fewest in number.

A. 21 CS · Communication, Information literacy

How many of your classmates have the following as their favourite sport? Find out.

Football	Cricket	Tennis	Table Tennis

B. 21 CS · Information literacy, Life Skills   CC · Integration with Environmental Studies

15 LIFE ON LAND

Aditi learnt that plants help us in many ways. Plants give us shade, clean the air and provide food. She bought some plant saplings from the nursery. She then made a list of different saplings that she bought.

Count and complete the table.

Snake plant	Cactus	Peace lily

C. 21 CS · Critical thinking   CC · Integration with English

Read the sentences.

I read 'Cinderella' on Monday. I read 'Little Red Riding Hood' on Wednesday. I read 'The Tortoise and Hare' on Friday. I did not read anything on Tuesday, Thursday, Saturday and Sunday.

Make a list of all the books that you have read. How many days does it take for you to finish reading a book?

SUSTAINABLE DEVELOPMENT GOALS

Question B is related to SDG 15 Life on Land. Do you plant saplings? Do you think we should plant more trees and saplings? Why? The answers to these questions would give you an idea about why plants are important for the life on land.

WORKSHEET 11

Count the insects and complete the data chart.

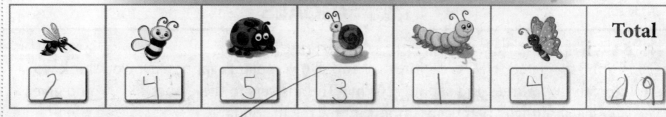						**Total**
2	4	5	3	1	4	19

Introduction to Multiplication

- To add objects in equal groups
- To relate repeated addition to the concept of multiplication
- To show repeated addition on the number line and understand skip counting

LET'S GET STARTED

21 CS | Critical thinking

Kriti and Jacob are baking cupcakes.

Help them put the 12 cupcakes on 6 plates. Each plate must have equal number of cupcakes.

There will be ___2___ cupcakes on each plate.

$$2 + 2 + 2 + 2 + 2 + 2 = 12$$

REPEATED ADDITION

We can add the same number over and over.

There are 3 groups. Each group has 3 starfish.

By adding the three numbers, we get

| 3 | 3 | 3 |

$3 + 3 + 3 = 9$

3 groups of 3

There are 9 starfish in all.

> Whenever we add the same number over and over, it is called repeated addition.

Example 1: Count the total number of groups and the total number of seashells.

2 groups of 4

DO YOU KNOW?
When a number is added to itself, it is a doubles fact.
$2 + 2$, $3 + 3$, $4 + 4$, ... are doubles facts.

Solution: There are two groups. Each group has 4 seashells.

Or, there are two groups of 4 seashells each.

$4 + 4 = 8$ seashells in all.

EXERCISE 12A

1. **Count the objects in each group and add.**

   a.

   _____8_____ + _____8_____ = ___16___

   There are __2__ groups of __8__ crabs each.
   There are __16__ crabs in all.

b.

_____3_____ + _____3_____

There are __2__ groups of __3__ balls each.
There are __6__ balls in all.

2. **Use repeated addition to complete the blanks.**

a.

_____5_____ + _____5_____ + _____5_____

3 groups of 5 ice creams each gives __15__ ice creams.

b.

_____4_____ + _____4_____ + _____4_____

3 groups of 4 sand castles each gives __12__ sand castles.

REPEATED ADDITION ON NUMBER LINE

When we count forward by a number other than 1, we skip count.

Counting in 2s gives the following pattern.

1	2	3	4	5	6	7	8	9	10

We can do the same using a number line.

Gary, the grasshopper, jumps 2 steps each time. What all numbers will Gary touch while jumping 4 times?

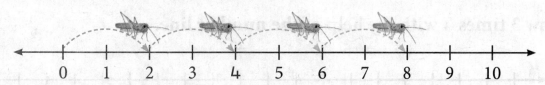

The grasshopper touched four numbers, **2, 4, 6** and **8**. So, we can say that 4 times 2 is equal to 8.

We have 2 + 2 + 2 + 2 = 8. The number 2 is repeatedly added 4 times. This can also be written as

$$4 \times 2 = 8$$

× is the sign for multiplication.
Multiplication means to add equal groups.

Example 2: Show 3 times 5 with the help of a number line.

Solution: Make 3 jumps of 5 from zero. You reach 15.

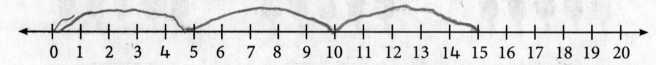

Therefore, 3 times 5 is 15.

COMMON ERRORS

Show 2 times 3 with the help of the number line.

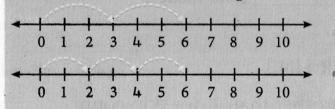

MENTAL MATHS

4 times 3 = 12
3 times 4 = 12
2 times 4 = 8
4 times 2 = 8

EXERCISE 12B

1. Show 2 times 6 with the help of the number line.

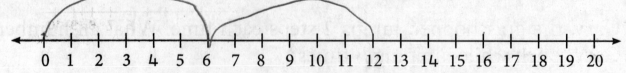

2. Show 3 times 4 with the help of the number line.

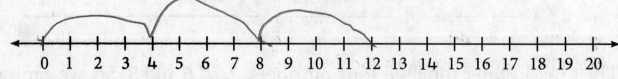

Aim: To visualise and understand repeated addition

Material required: A sheet of paper, *bindis*

Procedure:

1. Draw two vertical lines on a sheet of paper.
2. Draw a horizontal line that crosses the two vertical lines.
3. Paste *bindis* on the points where the two lines meet.
4. Again draw two vertical lines.
5. Now draw two horizontal lines that cross the two vertical lines.
6. Paste *bindis* on the points where these lines meet as shown alongside. This represents 2 + 2 = 4. Write this in your notebook.
7. Repeat the above steps by drawing 2 vertical lines and three horizontal lines, meeting at six points.
8. Continue the activity by increasing the number of horizontal lines one by one up to ten.
9. Write the repeated addition in your notebook.
10. Repeat the same activity with three vertical lines.

$2 + 2 = 4$

$2 + 2 + 2 = 6$

CONCEPT MAP

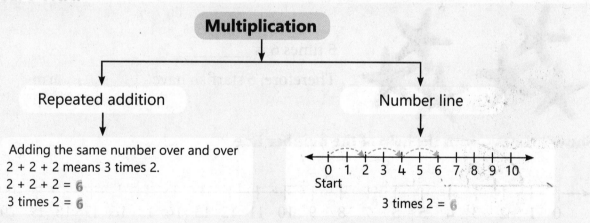

Multiplication

Repeated addition

Adding the same number over and over
2 + 2 + 2 means 3 times 2.
2 + 2 + 2 = 6
3 times 2 = 6

Number line

0 1 2 3 4 5 6 7 8 9 10
Start

3 times 2 = 6

KEY CONCEPTS

- **Repeated addition:** Adding the same number over and over
- **Skip count:** To count forward by a number other than 1
- **Multiplication:** To add equal groups

A. Look at the pictures and fill in the blanks.

1.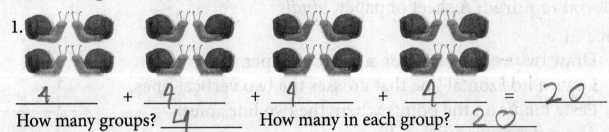

___4___ + ___4___ + ___4___ + ___4___ = ___20___

How many groups? ___4___   How many in each group? ___20___

There are ___20___ snails in all.

2.

___5___ + ___5___ = ___10___

How many groups? ___2___   How many in each group? ___10___

There are ___10___ shrimps in all.

B. Count by 5s and fill in the boxes given below.

5, 10 [15] [20] [25] [30] [35] [40] [45] [50]

C. A starfish has 5 arms.

5 times 6 is ___30___.

Therefore, 6 starfish have ___5___ arms.

D. Show 2 times 4 with the help of the number line.

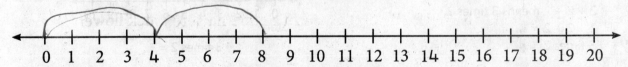

0 1 2 3 4 5 6 7 8 9 10 11 12 13 14 15 16 17 18 19 20

E. Show 4 times 5 with the help of the number line.

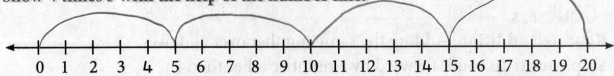

0 1 2 3 4 5 6 7 8 9 10 11 12 13 14 15 16 17 18 19 20

SKILL UP!

A. 21 CS) Critical thinking, Creativity and innovation   CC   Integration with English

Take 12 pencils. Arrange the pencils in rows in different ways. Each row must have the same number of pencils. Write repeated addition statements for three arrangements.

B. 21 CS) Life Skills   CC   Integration with Environmental Studies

Arnav and Hussain go for a walk. They see 5 plants in the garden. Each plant has 3 flowers.

How many flowers are there in all?
Arnav plucks all the three flowers from a plant. How many flowers are left now?

C. 21 CS) Critical thinking

Harmeet buys 7 pairs of socks from the market. How many socks has he bought altogether?

SUSTAINABLE DEVELOPMENT GOALS

Question B is related to SDG 15 Life on Land. Is it a good habit to pluck flowers? Think about it. Give reason for your answer.

WORKSHEET 12

Detective on the Job!

A few robbers are hiding in some flats of a locality. Help Detective Das to find these robbers. The given codes are the flat numbers where the robbers are hiding. Solve these codes. Give red colour to the boxes with flat numbers where the robbers are hiding.

Codes!

a. Four times three 12 b. Seven times two 14
c. Three times three 9 d. Three times seven 21
e. Four times four 16 f. Five times four 20

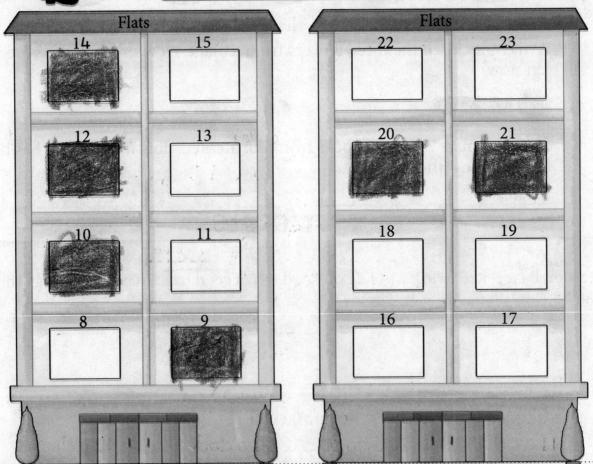

Flats

14	15
12	13
10	11
8	9

Flats

22	23
20	21
18	19
16	17

1. There are 79 teachers in a school. Jenny wants to give a flower to each teacher on Teacher's day. How many flowers will be needed?

   a. 30 + 32   b. 40 + 39   c. 35 + 23   d. 45 + 23

2. 15 children came to Dev's house for his birthday party. Dev's mother made a sandwich for each of them. How many sandwiches did his mother make?

   a. 75 – 60   b. 67 – 60   c. 56 – 42   d. 68 – 43

3. Arrange the teddy bears in ascending order of their heights.

   a. B < D < C < A
   b. A < C < B < D
   c. C < A < B < D
   d. D < C < B < A

4. Look at the images given below. Which is the lightest?

   a. Tomato   b. Strawberry   c. Pear   d. All are equal

5. What time did Ali finish his journey to reach his grandma's home? Use the clues given below to find out.

   _____9 a.m._____   _____   _____

   Ali started his journey at 9 o'clock in the morning.

   Ali spent 2 hours travelling in the train.

   He travelled for another 1 hour in a cab.

   a. 11 o'clock   b. 10 o'clock   c. 2 o'clock   d. 12 o'clock

Review 1

A. Look at the picture and fill in the blanks with the given words. (3 × 1)

right, left, longer

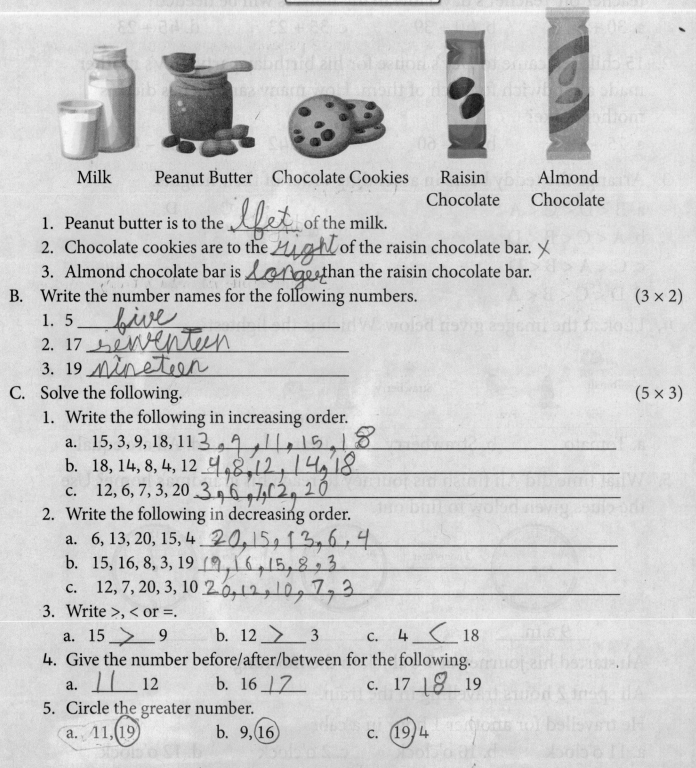

Milk   Peanut Butter   Chocolate Cookies   Raisin Chocolate   Almond Chocolate

1. Peanut butter is to the _lfet_ of the milk.
2. Chocolate cookies are to the _right_ of the raisin chocolate bar. ✗
3. Almond chocolate bar is _longer_ than the raisin chocolate bar.

B. Write the number names for the following numbers. (3 × 2)
1. 5 _five_
2. 17 _seventeen_
3. 19 _nineteen_

C. Solve the following. (5 × 3)
1. Write the following in increasing order.
   a. 15, 3, 9, 18, 11 _3, 9, 11, 15, 18_
   b. 18, 14, 8, 4, 12 _4, 8, 12, 14, 18_
   c. 12, 6, 7, 3, 20 _3, 6, 7, 12, 20_
2. Write the following in decreasing order.
   a. 6, 13, 20, 15, 4 _20, 15, 13, 6, 4_
   b. 15, 16, 8, 3, 19 _19, 16, 15, 8, 3_
   c. 12, 7, 20, 3, 10 _20, 12, 10, 7, 3_
3. Write >, < or =.
   a. 15 _>_ 9   b. 12 _>_ 3   c. 4 _<_ 18
4. Give the number before/after/between for the following.
   a. _11_ 12   b. 16 _17_   c. 17 _18_ 19
5. Circle the greater number.
   a. 11, (19)   b. 9, (16)   c. (19), 4

D. Solve the following word problems. (4 × 4)

1. There are 6 yellow butterflies sitting on a flower. Ten blue butterflies join them. How many butterflies are there in all? 16

2. If I read 7 pages of a book on one day and 3 pages of the same book the next day, how many pages did I read on both the days? 10

3. There are 12 books in one shelf. Kriti keeps 5 more books in the same shelf. How many books are there in the shelf now? 17

4. There are 13 children in a park. Four more children join them. How many children are there in total? 17

Rough Work

Maximum Marks = 40

A. Choose the correct option.   (3 × 1)

1. 8 − 3 = _5_

   a. 8   b. 3   c. 5   d. 2

2. Which shape will come next?

   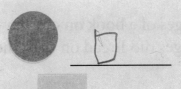   _____

   a.   b.   c.

3. 5 tens + 4 ones =

   a. 35   b. 45   c. 54   d. 21

B. Write the number names for the following numbers.   (3 × 2)

1. 55 _fifty five_
2. 87 _eight seven_
3. 99 _ninty nine_

C. Solve the following.   (5 × 3)

1. Subtract the following.

   a. 17 − 5 __12__
   b. 19 − 3 __16__
   c. 15 − 4 __11__ ✗

2. Write the number that comes in between.

   a. 79 _80_ 81   b. 62 _63_ 64   c. 56 _57_ 58

3. Add the following.

   a. 66 + 3 __69__
   b. 52 + 13 __65__
   c. 12 + 13 + 51 __76__

4. Write the greatest number and the smallest number for each of the following.

   a. 15, 79, 2   Greatest Number: __79__   Smallest Number: __2__
   b. 78, 42, 69   Greatest Number: __78__   Smallest Number: __42__
   c. 17, 85, 29   Greatest Number: __85__   Smallest Number: __17__

5. Subtract using the number line.

   17 − 2 = 15

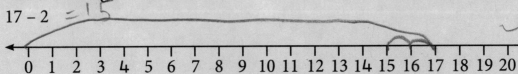

0 1 2 3 4 5 6 7 8 9 10 11 12 13 14 15 16 17 18 19 20

D. Answer the following questions. (4 × 4)

1. Circle the object that will come next.

2. Reena bought 8 chocolates. She ate 5 chocolates. How many chocolates were left with her? 3

3. If out of 15 pens I use 2 pens, how many pens will be left with me? 13

4. Neha bought 13 pink balloons and 25 blue balloons. How many balloons did Neha buy in total? 38

_____

Rough Work

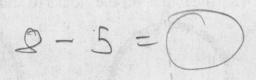

12
13
51

25
51
6

Review 3

A. Choose the correct option. (3 × 1)

1. 90 – 0 = __90__

   a. ✓ 90   b. 0   c. 80   d. 89

2.  +  = __10__

   a. ₹5   b. ₹55   c. ✓ ₹10   d. ₹15

3. 7 o'clock is also written as __07:00__

   a. ✓ 07:00   b. 08:00   c. 12:00   d. 6:00

B. Answer the following. (3 × 2)

1. First day of the week __Monday__

2. Last day of the week __Sunday__

3. Number of days in a week __7__

C. Solve the following. (5 × 3)

1. Tick the longest object.   2. Tick the one that holds more liquid.

3. Draw the hands on the clocks to show the given time.

   a.   b.   c.

   6:00   8:00   11:00

4. Write the value of the notes and coins given below.

   a.   b.   c.

   __5₹__   __2₹__   __20₹__

5. Solve the following.
   a. 65 – 24 ___41___
   b. 93 – 11 ___82___
   c. 84 – 21 ___73___

D. Answer the following questions. (4 × 4)

1. Out of 24 students in a class, 3 students were absent. How many students were present? 21

2. The teacher had 39 school diaries. She distributed 28 diaries to the students. How many diaries were left with her? 11

3. If I went to the park from 5 o'clock to 6 o'clock, how much time did I spend in the park? 1 hour

4. If I gave the shopkeeper a note of ₹50 and a note of ₹20, how much money did I give him? 70₹

_____

Rough Work

$$
\begin{array}{r} 65 \\ -24 \\ \hline 41 \end{array}
\qquad
\begin{array}{r} 93 \\ -11 \\ \hline 82 \end{array}
\qquad
\begin{array}{r} 84 \\ -21 \\ \hline 73 \end{array}
$$

A. Choose the correct option. (3 × 1)

1. There are __2__ groups of __3__ ice creams.

    a. ✓ 2, 3   b. 3, 2   c. ✓ 3, 3

2. Which of the following shows the correct repeated addition?

    a. 7 + 7   b. 3 + 7   c. ✓ 6 + 6 + 6

3. 5 times 2 = __10__

    a. 8   b. 14   c. 10

B. Do as directed.

1. Draw 4 groups of 3 ▮▮▮ each. Then use repeated addition to find how many blue rectangles are there in all. = __12__ (3 × 2)

2. Complete the following.
    a. 5 + 5 + 5 + 5 = __4__ times __5__ = 20
    b. 3 + 3 + 3 + 3 = __4__ times __3__ = 12

3. State true or false.
    a. 4 groups of 2 is 4 + 4. _false_ 2 + 2 + 2 + 2
    b. 2 groups of 6 is 12. _true_

C. Solve the following. (5 × 3)

1. Look at the picture and answer the following questions.

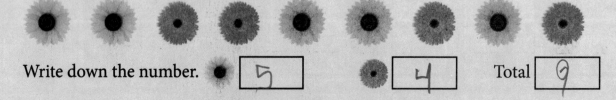

    Write down the number. ● __5__   ● __4__   Total __9__

2. Fill in the blanks.

   a. 3 + 3 = 2 times = 6

   b. 5 + 5 + 5 = 3 times 3

   c. 4 + 4 + 4 = 3 times 3

3. An octopus has 8 arms. How many arms do 3 octopuses have?

   8 + 8 + 8 = 3 times 8 = 24

4. Solve the following.

   a. 5 times 4 = 20

   b. 2 times 6 = 12

   c. 4 times 3 = 12

5. Represent 4 times 2 on the number line.

4 times 2 = 4 × 2 = 8

D. Answer the following questions.   (4 × 4)

   1. Look at the objects and answer the following.

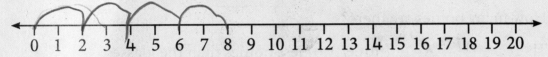

   Total number of objects = 14

   Count each type of object and fill in the boxes.

   Tick (✓) the one which is the most in number.

   Cross (✗) the one which is the fewest in number.

   a.  5   b. 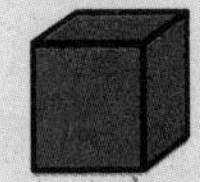 X   c.  ✓

2. Look at the items and answer the following.

    a. How many items are there in all? ___12___

    b. How many bottles are there? ___3___

    c. There are ___two___ (three/two) less bottles than the glasses.

    d. The number of ___glass___ is the greatest in number.

3. Show the following on the number line.

    a. 2 times 4

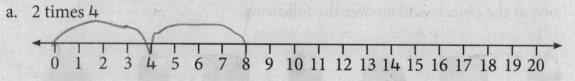

    b. 5 times 3

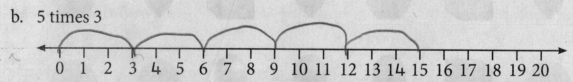

4. Count the objects in each group and add.

    a. There are ___2___ groups of ___3___ pencils each.
    b. There are ___9___ pencils in all.
    c. 3 times 3 = ___9___

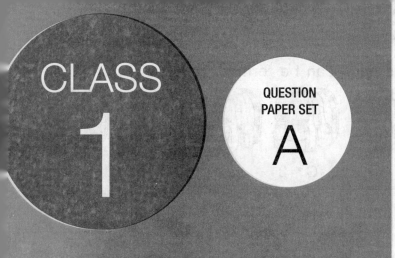

CLASS 1

QUESTION PAPER SET A

SOF INTERNATIONAL MATHEMATICS OLYMPIAD 2020-21

DO NOT OPEN THIS BOOKLET UNTIL ASKED TO DO SO

Total Questions: 35 | Time: 1 hr.

Guidelines for the Candidate

You will get additional ten minutes to fill up information about yourself on the OMR Sheet, before the start of the exam.

Write your **Name, School Code, Class, Section, Roll No.** and **Mobile Number** clearly on the **OMR Sheet** and do not forget to sign it. We will share your marks / result and other information related to SOF exams on your mobile number.

The Question Paper comprises four sections:

Logical Reasoning (10 Questions), **Mathematical Reasoning** (10 Questions), **Everyday Mathematics** (10 Questions) and **Achievers Section** (5 Questions)

Each question in Achievers Section carries 2 marks, whereas all other questions carry one mark each.

All questions are compulsory. There is no negative marking. Use of calculator is not permitted.

There is only ONE correct answer. Choose only ONE option for an answer.

To mark your choice of answers by darkening the circles on the OMR Sheet, use **HB Pencil** or **Blue / Black ball point pen** only. E.g.

Q.16: Sonia had 80 sweets. She gave 15 sweets to Danish and 15 sweets to Megha. How many sweets are left with her?

A. 50   B. 30   C. 60   D. 40

As the correct answer is option A, you must darken the circle corresponding to option A on the OMR Sheet.

Rough work should be done in the blank space provided in the booklet.

Return the OMR Sheet to the invigilator at the end of the exam.

Please fill in your personal details in the space provided on this page before attempting the paper.

SOF
SCIENCE OLYMPIAD FOUNDATION
Inspiring Young Minds Through Knowledge Olympiads

Name:...

Section:.......... SOF Olympiad Roll No.:.. Contact No.:...

1. There are ___2___ groups of 4 bags each can be formed from the given bags.

   A. 1   B. 2 ✓   C. 3   D. 4

2. Who is at the first position?

   A. Saumya
   B. Rohit
   C. Harish
   D. ✓ Anju

   Saumya   Rohit   Harish   Anju

3. Which of the following options will complete the pattern in the given figure?

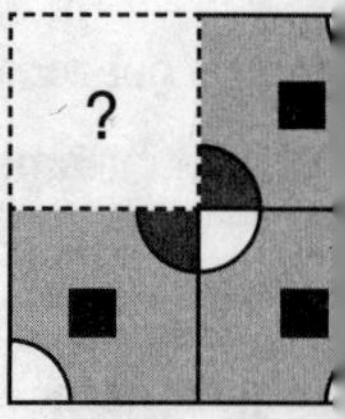

   A.  ✓   B.

   C. 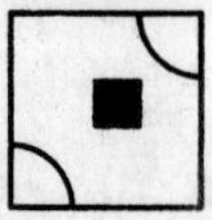   D.

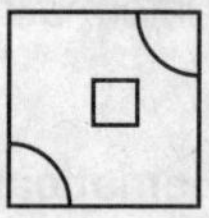

4. Shapes ___P___ and ___R___ will form a square.

   P   Q   R   S

   A. P and Q   B. ✓ P and R   C. Q and R   D. P and S

5. ___Sea___ is the shortest.

   A.    B.    C.    D.

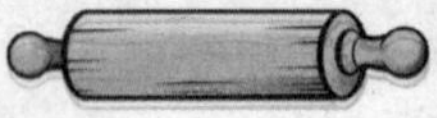

6. Which of the following will complete the given number pattern?

   3   6   9   12   ( )   18   21

   A. 13   B. ✓ 15   C. ✓ 21   D. 24

SPACE FOR ROUGH WORK

7. If Kartik's birthday falls on 4th Tuesday of January 20XX, then on which date will he celebrate his birthday?

A. 14th January

B. 7th January

C. ✓ 28th January

D. 27th January

JANUARY 20XX

Sun	Mon	Tue	Wed	Thu	Fri	Sat
			1	2	3	4
5	6	7	8	9	10	11
12	13	14	15	16	17	18
19	20	21	22	23	24	25
26	27	28	29	30	31	

8. _Cake_ is kept on the table.

A. ✓ Cake

B. Cat

C. Ball

D. Birthday cap

9. is related to , in the same way as is related to _A_ .

A.  ✓

B.

C.

D.

10. Which of the following objects can roll but not slide?

A.

B.

C ✓

D.

MATHEMATICAL REASONING

11. Which of the following abacuses shows 14 more than 24?

A.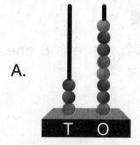

B.

C.

D.

SPACE FOR ROUGH WORK

12. If 1 ▭ means 1 unit, then the toothbrush is _7_ units long.

A. 17   B. 7   C. 12   D. 8

13. Identify the number.

A. 89

B. 81

C. 91

D. 94

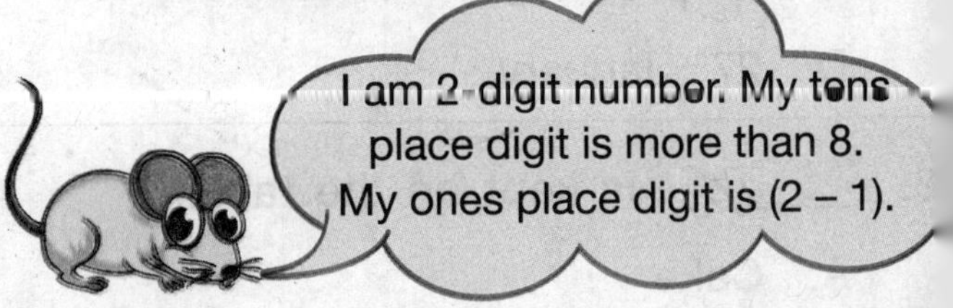

I am 2-digit number. My tens place digit is more than 8. My ones place digit is (2 – 1).

14. The given weighing scale shows _A_.

A. Puppy is heavier than bat

B. Puppy is lighter than bat

C. Both have the same weight

D. Can't be determined

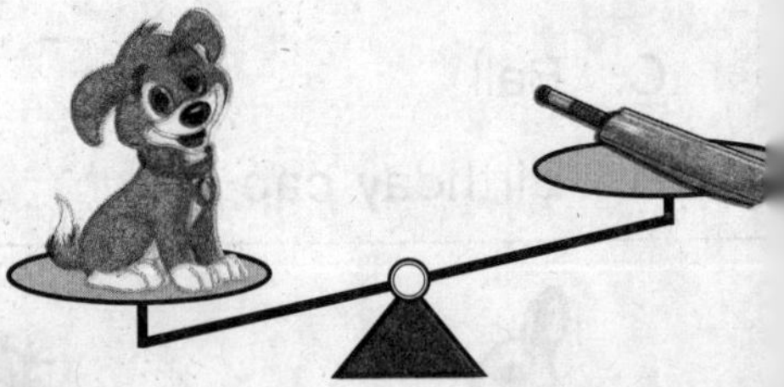

15. How many more lamps should be crossed to make the given subtraction sentence TRUE

'15 – 6'

A. 3   B. 4   C. 5   D. 6

16. The number of candies shown here is _____.

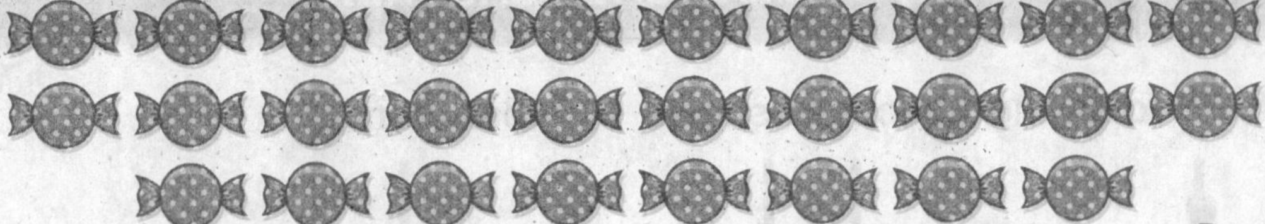

A. 2 tens 1 ones   B. 1 tens 8 ones   C. 1 tens 5 ones   D. 2 tens 8 ones

17. There are _6_ months lie between May and November.

A. 4   B. 5   C. 6   D. 3

SPACE FOR ROUGH WORK

T O
9 1

162

8. Find the value of P + Q. $P = 3 \quad Q = 3$

A. 3

B. 4

C. 5

D. ✓ 6

	2	P
+	Q	1
	5	4

9. Which of the following sets has the same number of objects as in the given set?

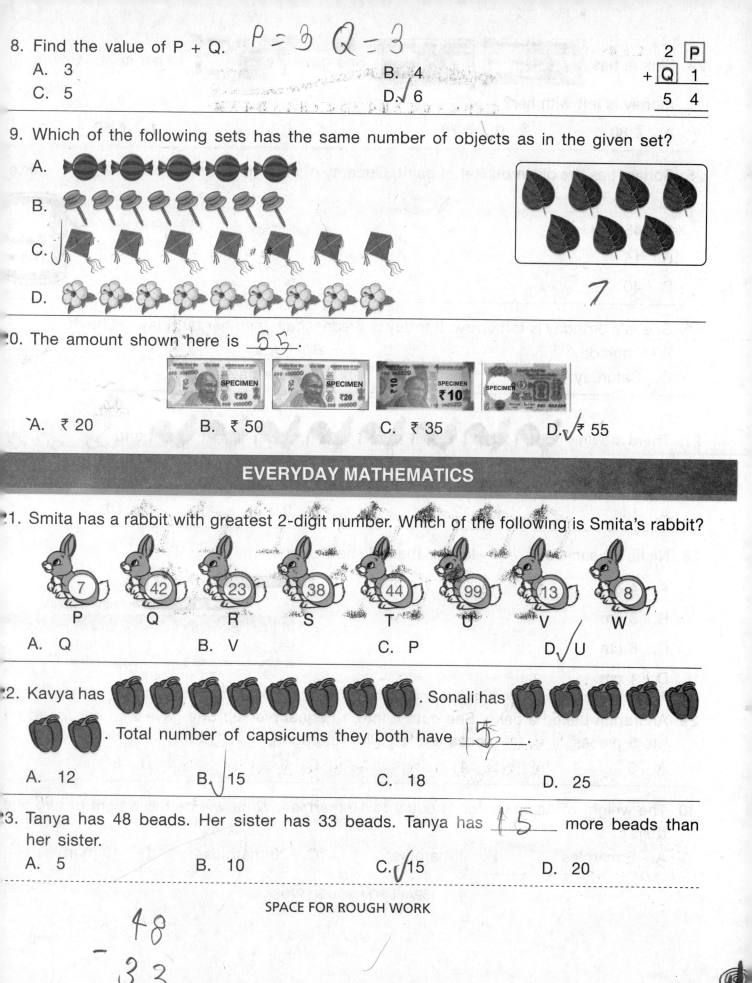

A.

B.

C. ✓

D.

7

20. The amount shown here is _55_.

A. ₹ 20

B. ₹ 50

C. ₹ 35

D. ✓ ₹ 55

EVERYDAY MATHEMATICS

21. Smita has a rabbit with greatest 2-digit number. Which of the following is Smita's rabbit?

7   42   23   38   44   99   13   8
P   Q   R   S   T   U   V   W

A. Q

B. V

C. P

D. ✓ U

22. Kavya has   . Sonali has

. Total number of capsicums they both have _15_.

A. 12

B. ✓ 15

C. 18

D. 25

23. Tanya has 48 beads. Her sister has 33 beads. Tanya has _15_ more beads than her sister.

A. 5

B. 10

C. ✓ 15

D. 20

SPACE FOR ROUGH WORK

48
- 33

24. Shikha has . She gave to her sister. How muc money is left with her?

   A. ₹ 80   B. ₹ 70   C. ₹ 60   D. ₹ 50

25. Soham has the given bucket of paint. Quantity of paint in 3 such buckets is 45 ___ litre

   A. 30
   B. 45
   C. 15
   D. 40

26. Sneha's birthday is tomorrow. If today is Wednesday, then her birthday will be on _____

   A. Thursday   B. Friday
   C. Saturday   D. Tuesday

27. There are only and

   in a farm. How many total birds are there in the farm?

   A. 14   B. 12   C. 9   D. 10

28. Nisha's pencil is __1 cm__ longer than Misha's pencil.   6 − 5 = 1

   A. 4 cm
   B. 3 cm
   C. 8 cm
   D. 1 cm

29. Anuradha baked a cake. She cuts it into 10 equal pieces. She gave 2 to her friend an ate 5 pieces. ___3___ pieces are left with Anuradha.

   A. 3   B. 4   C. 6   D. 8

30. The weight of Aastha's doll is equal to 10 marbles. What will be the weight of two suc dolls?

   A. 5 marbles   B. 2 marbles   C. 20 marbles   D. 10 marbles

SPACE FOR ROUGH WORK

120
− 50
70

15
+ 15
+ 15

15

31. If + = ₹ 108 and = ₹ 36, then = ₹ _72_ .

   A. 70   B. 72   C. 36   D. 58

32. Select the CORRECT statement.
   A.   If 10 is added to 20, then the result will be 28.
   B.   The number lies between 28 and 30 is 29.
   C.   9 tens + 3 ones = 98
   D.   5 less than 98 is 9 tens 5 ones.

33. Which of the following options has value 28?

A.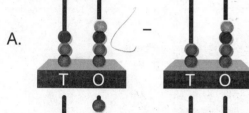

B.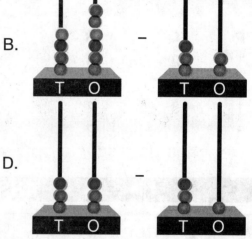

C.

D.

34. Study the figure carefully.

   P   Q   R   S   T   U   V   W

(a)   Car ___P___ is farthest from the given parking board.
(b)   Car ___T___ is at fourth position from the given parking board.

	(a)	(b)
A.	P	T
B.	P	S
C.	W	T
D.	W	S

SPACE FOR ROUGH WORK

108
- 36
 72

35. Match the following and select the CORRECT option.

Column-1   Column-2

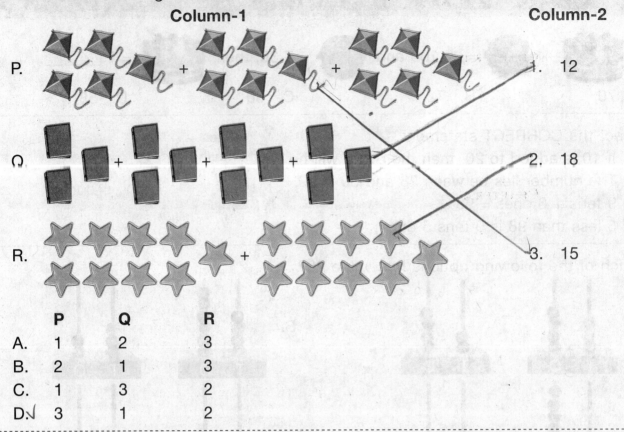

P.

Q.

R.

	P	**Q**	**R**
A.	1	2	3
B.	2	1	3
C.	1	3	2
D.✓	3	1	2

ANSWER KEYS

1.	(B)	2.	(D)	3.	(A)	4.	(B)	5.	(C)	6.	(B)	7.	(C)
8.	(A)	9.	(A)	10.	(C)	11.	(A)	12.	(B)	13.	(C)	14.	(A)
15.	(A)	16.	(D)	17.	(B)	18.	(D)	19.	(C)	20.	(D)	21.	(D)
22.	(B)	23.	(C)	24.	(B)	25.	(B)	26.	(A)	27.	(B)	28.	(D)
29.	(A)	30.	(C)	31.	(B)	32.	(B)	33.	(C)	34.	(A)	35.	(D)

SOF INTERNATIONAL GENERAL KNOWLEDGE OLYMPIAD

SOF INTERNATIONAL ENGLISH OLYMPIAD

SOF NATIONAL SCIENCE OLYMPIAD

SOF INTERNATIONAL MATHEMATICS OLYMPIAD

For latest updates & information, please like 👍 our Facebook page (www.facebook.com/sofworld) or register o

http://www.sofworld.org/subscribe-updates.html

For Level 1 and Level 2 preparation material / free sample papers, please log on to www.mtg.in

SCIENCE OLYMPIAD FOUNDATION

National Office: Plot 99, First Floor, Sector 44 Institutional area, Gurugram -122 003 (HR) India
Email: info@sofworld.org | Website: www.sofworld.org
Regd. Office: 406, Taj Apt., Ring Road, New Delhi-110 029
Note: Please address all communication to the National Office only.

Answers

CHAPTER 1

Pre-Number Skills

Chapter Revision

A. 1. on   2. near   3. far   4. under

B. 1. up   2. down   3. after   4. before

   5. between

CHAPTER 2

Numbers up to 20

Exercise 2A

1. a. Colour 9 papayas   b. Colour 6 mangoes

2. a. 3   b. 4   c. 9   d. 7

3. a. C   b. D   c. B   d. A

Exercise 2B

2.

	Number	Number Name
a.	11	Eleven
b.	13	Thirteen
c.	15	Fifteen
d.	17	Seventeen
e.	14	Fourteen

3. b.

Tens	Ones
1	8

c.

Tens	Ones
1	5

d.

Tens	Ones
1	7

Exercise 2C

  1. after   2. after   3. between   4. before

Exercise 2D

1. a. 19, 5, 7, 1, 6

   The increasing order is 1, 5, 6, 7, 19.

   The decreasing order is 19, 7, 6, 5, 1.

  b. 15, 18, 13, 17, 11

   The increasing order is 11, 13, 15, 17, 18.

   The deceasing order is 18, 17, 15, 13, 11.

2. a. 5 < 9   b. 12 > 10   c. 19 > 11

3. a. Greatest number: 9; red

   Smallest number: 2; yellow

  b. Greatest number: 19; red

   Smallest number: 11; yellow

4. a.

  b.

Chapter Revision

A.

	Number	Number Name
1.	3	Three
2.	5	Five
3.	10	Ten
4.	16	Sixteen
5.	9	Nine

B. 1. 19, 1, 8, 15, 12

   The increasing order is 1, 8, 12, 15, 19.

   The decreasing order is 19, 15, 12, 8, 1.

  2. 5, 20, 13, 8, 16

   The increasing order is 5, 8, 13, 16, 20

   The decreasing order is 20, 16, 13, 8, 5

C. 16, 7, 13

D. 1. >   2. =

E. 1. Greatest number: 17; red

   Smallest number: 7; yellow

  2. Greatest number: 20; red

   Smallest number: 4; yellow

CHAPTER 3

Addition up to 20

Exercise 3A

  1. 5   2. 7   3. 7   4. 8   5. 9

Exercise 3B

1. a.

4 + 3 = 7

  b.

1 + 3 = 4

  c.

2 + 5 = 7

  d.

5 + 4 = 9

  e.

3 + 6 = 9

2. a. 8   b. 2   c. 8   d. 6
    e. 9   f. 1   g. 9   h. 6

Exercise 3C

1. 1 red crayon + 2 green crayons = 3 crayons, 3

2. 5 red apples + 2 green apples = 7 apples, 7

3. 6 cookies + 3 cookies = 9 cookies, 9

4. 4 butterflies + 2 butterflies = 6 butterflies, 6

Exercise 3D

1. a. 18   b. 19   c. 10   d. 7
    e. 19   f. 16

2. a.

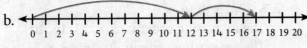

$6 + 3 = 9$

b.

$12 + 5 = 17$

Exercise 3E

1. 6   2. 8   3. 9   4. 13
5. 15   6. 14

Exercise 3F

1. 16   2. 11   3. 17   4. 19

Chapter Revision

A. 1. 16   2. 18   3. 18   4. 13
    5. 15   6. 12

B.

$6 + 7 = 13$

C. 19 birds   D. 18 cars

CHAPTER 4

Subtraction up to 20

Exercise 4A

1. 3   2. 4   3. 5   4. 5
5. 5   6. 1   7. 4

Exercise 4B

1. b. 2, 3, 4, 5; 3   c. 4, 5, 6; 2

2. b. 2, 3, 4, 5, 6, 7, 8, 9
    $9 - 7 = 2$
    ②, 3, 4, 5, 6, 7, 8, 9

    c. 1, 2, 3, 4, 5
    $5 - 4 = 1$
    ①, 2, 3, 4, 5

Exercise 4C

1. a.

$5 - 3 = 2$

b.

$4 - 2 = 2$

c.

$7 - 1 = 6$

d.

$8 - 0 = 8$

2. a. 5   b. 5   c. 9   d. 3   e. 4   f. 7

3. b. ⓺ − 2 = 4 = ⑧ − 4   c. ⑩ − 5 = 5 = ⑥ − 1
    d. ⑨ − 6 = 3 = ⑤ − 2   e. ③ − 1 = 2 = ⑥ − 4

Exercise 4D

1. a. 11   b. 13   c. 12   d. 11   e. 13   f. 17

2. a. 4   b. 12   c. 10   d. 11   e. 0 /Zero

Chapter Revision

A. 1. 11   2. 12   3. 14   4. 12   5. 15   6. 10

B. 1.

$18 - 9 = 9$

2.

$12 - 7 = 5$

C. 10 cars

D. 13 cakes

CHAPTER 5

Shapes and Patterns

Exercise 5A

1. a. Image 2   b. Image 1   c. Image 3   d. Image 2

2. a. Shapes 1 and 4 are circles

    b. Shapes 1 and 5 are rectangles

    c. Shapes 2 and 5 are triangles

3. a. Image 2 of circle

    b. Image 2 of rectangle

    c. Image 4 of triangle

Exercise 5B

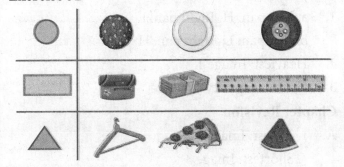

Exercise 5C

1.

2.

3.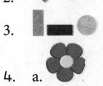

4. a.   b.

Chapter Revision

A. 1. Colour the triangle shapes 1, 3 and 4
    2. Colour the circle shapes 1 and 4
    3. Colour the square shapes 2 and 5
    4. Colour the rectangle shapes 1 and 4

B. 1.    2.

C. 1. Shapes 2, 5 and 6
    2. Shapes 1, 3, 4 and 6

D. 1.   2.

CHAPTER 6

Numbers up to 100

Exercise 6A

1. a. 22   b. 34   c. 44   d. 33
    e. 47   f. 38
2. a. 2 tens 0 ones   b. 3 tens 9 ones
    c. 2 tens 6 ones   d. 4 tens 4 ones

Exercise 6B

1. 62, 63, 64, 65, 66, 67, 68, 69, 70, 71, 72, 73, 74, 75, 76, 77, 78, 79, 80, 81, 82, 83, 84, 85, 86, 87, 88, 89
2. a. Twenty-three   b. Thirty-eight
    c. Forty-two   d. Seventy-eight
    e. Ninety-four

Exercise 6C

1. a. 70, 4   b. 60, 1
2. a. 50 + 4   b. 60 + 7   c. 80 + 3
3. a. 44   b. 92   c. 86
4. a. 68   b. 84   c. 95
5. a. 79   b. 60   c. 92

Exercise 6D

1. >   2. <   3. >   4. <   5. =   6. >

Exercise 6E

1. 89
2. 8
3. a. 7, 19, 23, 65, 84   b. 2, 14, 35, 68, 79
4. a. 83, 72, 24, 19, 5   b. 78, 69, 42, 35, 1

Chapter Revision

A. 1. Twenty-three   2. Thirty-nine
    3. Forty-seven   4. Fifty-six

B. 1. 43   2. 76   3. 92   4. 58
    5. 71   6. 58

C. 1. 32   2. 47, 48, 49
    3. 72, 73, 74   4. 93, 94, 95

D. 1. Greatest: 90, Smallest: 7
    2. Greatest: 82, Smallest: 23

E. 52, 28, 34

F. 92, 71, 88

G. 1. 8, 12, 23, 52, 97   2. 12, 21, 67, 85, 92

H. 1. 71, 69, 58, 26, 21   2. 78, 52, 43, 12, 8

I. 1. 50, 60, 70, 80   2. 15, 18, 21, 24

CHAPTER 7

Addition up to 99

Exercise 7A

1. 50   2. 60   3. 70   4. 80
5. 90   6. 90   7. 90   8. 60
9. 60

Exercise 7B

1. 25   2. 75   3. 58   4. 49
5. 89   6. 98

Exercise 7C

1. 37   2. 99   3. 81   4. 97
5. 78   6. 99

Exercise 7D

1. 89   2. 68   3. 37   4. 59

Chapter Revision

A. 1. 38   2. 99   3. 96   4. 67
   5. 86   6. 89

B. 59

C. 48

D. 1. 59   2. 68   3. 78   4. 78
   5. 87   6. 86

CHAPTER 8

Subtraction up to 99

Exercise 8A

1. a. 40   b. 50   c. 80   d. 50
   e. 20   f. 50   g. 10   h. 30

2. a. 67   b. 47   c. 83   d. 79

Exercise 8B

1. 21   2. 35   3. 63   4. 12
5. 72   6. 41   7. 11   8. 39
9. 20   10. 52   11. 41   12. 25

Exercise 8C

1. 24   2. 42   3. 31   4. 32

Chapter Revision

A. 1. 10   2. 80

B. 1. b   2. c   3. a   4. d

C. 1. 42   2. 31   3. 25   4. 33
   5. 7   6. 31

D. 26

E. 14

CHAPTER 9

Measurement

Exercise 9A

1. a. Answer may vary.   b. Answer may vary.
   c. Answer may vary.

2. a. Longest: Image 2
   b. Longest: Image 1
   c. Longest: Image 3
   d. Longest: Image 2

3. a. Tallest: Image 1
      Shortest: Image 3
   b. Tallest: Image 3
      Shortest: Image 1

Exercise 9B

1. a. Left pan: H; Right pan: L
   b. Left pan: L; Right pan: H

2. Heaviest: Image 1

3. Greater capacity: Image 1

Chapter Revision

A. 1. Tallest: Image 1
      Shortest: Image 3
   2. Tallest: Image 2
      Shortest: Image 3

B. 1. Screwdriver: 12 blocks
   2. Spoon: 10 blocks

C. 1. Left pan: H; Right pan: L
   2. Left pan: L; Right pan: H
   3. Left pan: H; Right pan: L

D. 1. Image 1: M; Image 2: L
   2. Image 1: L; Image 2: M

CHAPTER 10

Time and Money

Exercise 10A

1. a. 12, 5, 5:00 or 5 o'clock
   b. 12, 7, 7:00 or 7 o'clock
   c. 12, 1, 1:00 or 1 o'clock

2. a.   b.

   c.

3. a.   b.

   c.

Exercise 10B

1. a. Monday   b. Saturday
   c. Tuesday   d. Wednesday

2. a. Washing the car

   b. Baking a cake

   c. Reading a story book

Exercise 10C

   1. ₹8   2. ₹25   3. ₹29   4. ₹6

Chapter Revision

A. 1.   2.

   3.   4.

B. 2. 6:00, 6 o'clock   3. 8:00, 8 o'clock

C. 1. ₹2   2. ₹5   3. ₹20   4. ₹50

D. ₹15 = ₹5 + ₹2 + ₹2 + ₹1 + ₹5

   ₹20 = ₹5 + ₹5 + ₹10

CHAPTER 11

Data Handling

Chapter Revision

A.
Fruit	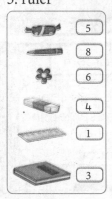				
Number	6	5	4	4	3

   1. Orange   2. Cherry

   3. 22 fruits

B. 1. 27   2. 4   3. 3   4. less

   5. ruler

CHAPTER 12

Introduction to Multiplication

Exercise 12A

1. 8 + 8 = 16; 2, 8; 16   2. 3 + 3 = 6; 2, 3; 6

2. a. 5 + 5 + 5 = 15; 3 groups of 5 = 15

   b. 4 + 4 + 4 = 12; 3 groups of 4 = 12

Exercise 12B

1.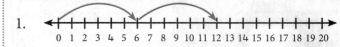

2 times 6 = 2 × 6 = 12

2.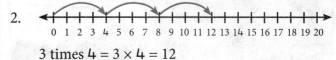

3 times 4 = 3 × 4 = 12

Chapter Revision

A. 1. 4 + 4 + 4 + 4 = 16

   4 groups; 4 in each group; 16

   2. 5 + 5 = 10

   2 groups; 5 in each group; 10

B. 15, 20, 25, 30, 35, 40, 45, 50

C. 5 times 6 = 5 × 6 = 30, 30 arms

D.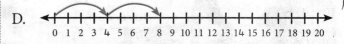

2 times 4 = 2 × 4 = 8

E.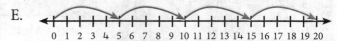

4 times 5 = 4 × 5 = 20

Honesty Is the Best Policy!

Rita and Larry's mother bought 20 chocolate muffins.

Larry, Rita, I have chocolate muffins for you. Wash your hands and come here.

Here are 3 muffins for each of you. This is a reward for keeping your room clean.

Yay! Thank you Mummy. These are my favourite!

They look yummy!

The next day…

Children, yesterday we had 20 muffins. Now, there are only 10. Have you taken any?

Sorry Mummy, I forgot to tell you. Yesterday, Palit came over. I shared 2 muffins with him.

Rita, Larry is honest. He told me that he had taken muffins. Did you take any?

No, Mummy, I did not. Larry must have taken more.

Mother takes Rita to her bedroom.

Rita, it's okay to take food if you want to eat something tasty. But it is dishonest to lie about it.

I am sorry, Mummy. I could not help myself. I took just 1 muffin in the noon and 1 in the evening.

172

My SEE (Social Emotional Ethical) Space

A. Answer the following questions.

1. How many muffins did the mother give to her children in all?

_____

2. How many muffins were left in the jar after the mother gave the muffins to her children?

_____

3. How many muffins did Rita eat in the whole day?

_____

B. Who was honest and who was dishonest? Do you think being honest is important? Share your thoughts in the space below.

_____

_____

C. Discuss the importance of honesty with your parents. Write the main points of your discussion in the box.

Maths Mela

Let us build your dream house.

All You Need Is... Sheets of coloured marble paper, tracing paper, pair of scissors, white chart paper and glue

Let's Start!

Note:
Do not use scissors or cutter yourself. Take help of an elder while cutting.

1 Draw an outline of your house on a white chart paper.

2 The front face of the house can be a rectangle. The roof can be a triangle. The door can also be a rectangle, and the windows can be squares.

3 On both sides of the house, draw some trees. The top of the trees can be circles and the stems can be triangles. Draw a circle in the sky for the Sun.

4 Now, place the tracing paper on each shape and trace the outlines.

5 Put the traced paper on the marble paper of your colour choice and trace its outline. It leaves an impression on the marble paper. Now outline it with a pencil.

6

Cut the shapes drawn on marble paper. Paste these over the shapes that are drawn on white chart paper with the help of glue.

7 Colour the remaining part of the white chart paper with crayons.

8 Your dream house is ready.

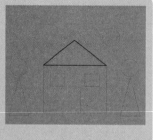

Do It Yourself!

Write the name of the shapes used to build your dream house. Also, count and write the number of each shape.

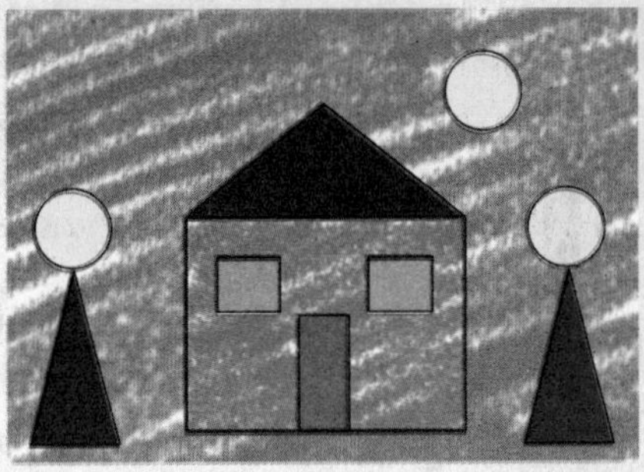

_____
_____
_____
_____
_____
_____

Make and colour a model of the village using different shapes. Draw a scene of the village you would make in the box given below. Write the materials required and the steps to construct the model.

All I Need Is: _____
_____
_____
_____

Let's Start: _____
_____
_____
_____
_____
_____
_____
_____
_____
_____
_____
_____
_____
_____
_____

Eminent Mathematicians

ARYABHATA (476–550 AD)

Aryabhata is one of the most famous mathematicians who brought new theories in mathematics. He also played a very major role in determining the place value system and discovering zero. He is also regarded as the first mathematician to use zero in the place value system. Aryabhata stated the total number of days in a year correctly, that is, 365. He was the first person to mention that the Earth was not flat but in fact spherical in shape.

 10, 100, 1000, 10000, …

BRAHMAGUPTA (597–668 AD)

Brahmagupta was a highly accomplished ancient Indian mathematician who gave four methods of multiplication. His main contribution was the introduction of zero and rules to compute with zero. He stated the fact that zero (0) stood for 'nothing' in the world of mathematics and treated zero as a number in its own right. He established the basic mathematical rules for dealing with zero $(1 + 0 = 1; 1 - 0 = 1;$ and $1 \times 0 = 0)$.

$$1 + 0 = 1, \quad 1 - 0 = 1, \quad 1 \times 0 = 0$$

BLAISE PASCAL
(19 JUNE 1623–19 AUGUST 1662)

Blaise Pascal invented a mechanical calculator at the age of 19. Known as the 'Arithmetic Machine'; then the 'Pascaline'; this machine assisted in the direct addition and subtraction of two numbers, and multiplication and division by repetition.

ALAN TURING
(23 JUNE 1912–7 JUNE 1954)

Alan Turing used mathematics theories and principles to formulate computations for a computer, called the Turing Machine. He used his mathematical knowledge and devised techniques that helped in code breaking. He is known as father of modern computing.

SHAKUNTALA DEVI (4 NOVEMBER 1929–21 APRIL 2013)

Shakuntala Devi is known as a 'Human Computer' because of her extraordinary talents in solving complex mathematical problems without any mechanical aid. On 18 June 1980, Shakuntala Devi multiplied two 13-digit figures within 28 seconds. She found her place in the Guinness book of records because of her extraordinary talents.

$$7,686,369,774,870 \times 2,465,099,745,779$$
$$= 18,947,668,177,995,426,462,773,730$$

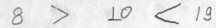

Times Tabl[es]

Skills

Exercises devised by Michael Tonge
an experienced mathematics teacher
Illustrated by Kelly Dooley

AGE
9

Times Tables Skills 8-9 forms part of **Learning Rewards**, a home-learning programme designed to help your child succeed at school with the National Curriculum. It has been extensively researched with children and teachers.

This book stands alone as a support for times tables for this age group, but is also a natural follow-on to *Times Tables Skills 7-8*. The companion titles, *Mathematics Skills* and *Adding and Subtracting Skills* complete the programme for Key Stage 2 numeracy.

Times tables are made easy in the following pages, through the use of novel and memorable teaching methods, and through repetition of ideas. You can help your child in his or her learning by helping to visualise the practice of multiplication and division. Grouping everyday, household objects together and then physically dividing them up again is a simple and constructive way to demonstrate the working out of a sum or problem. Many other practical teaching tips are found throughout the book.

The level of the exercises is progressive in this book, so try to work through them in order. It is important to stop before your child has had enough and to return at a later date to any exercise that he or she is struggling with.

The fold-out progress chart is a useful record of your child's performance and helps identify his or her strengths and weaknesses. Always reward your child's work with lots of encouragement and a gold star.

When you come to the end of the book, you will find a fun, wipe-clean learning game.

Key to symbols on the page:

 skills covered by each exercise as they relate to the National Curriculum

 notes for parents, explaining specific teaching points

 follow-up activities which will extend your child's understanding of the exercise

commissioning editor: Nina Filipek series editor: Stephanie Sloan
designer: Liz Brown cover design: Paul Dronsfield
Copyright © 1999 World International Limited.
All rights reserved.
Published in Great Britain by
World International Limited, Deanway Technology Centre,
Wilmslow Road, Handforth, Cheshire SK9 3FB.
Printed in Italy
ISBN 0 7498 4021 8

WORLD

Multiplication rules

To learn to solve tables problems, spotting rules for multiplication.

Fill in these multiplication squares.

x	3	5	1	7	9
9					
7					
5					
3					
1					

x	2	6	4	8	10
10					
2					
4					
6					
8					

x	1	2	5	3	7
3					
4					
8					
10					
6					

x	2	3	4	5	6
7					
8					
9					
10					
2					

Look at your answers and then complete these sentences.

An odd number times an odd number gives an _____ number.

An odd number times an even number gives an _____ number.

An even number multiplied by an even number gives an _____ number.

A number multiplied by 5 always ends in ___ or ___ .

A number multiplied by 10 always ends in ___ .

 Encourage your child to look for patterns in the numbers and identify the simple rules of multiplication.

 Draw a grid or write out the tables and ask your child to find as many patterns as possible, e.g. the tens and units pattern of the 9 times table.

2

To learn to solve simple multiplication sums and problems, using all the tables.

Multiplication with all tables

Can you solve these multiplication sums and problems?

1. 1 x 10 = ☐

2. 4 x 7 = ☐

3. 3 x 5 = ☐

4. 10 x 6 = ☐

5. 4 x 8 = ☐

6. 8 x 3 = ☐

7. 6 x 9 = ☐

8. 7 x 2 = ☐

9. 2 x 4 = ☐

10. 8 x 6 = ☐

If 12 people each bring 8 cakes to a party, how many cakes are there?_____

If 4 teams of 8 people each need a pair of gloves to have a snowball fight, how many gloves do they need altogether?_____

11 five-a-side football teams are playing out in the snow. Each player needs a warm drink. How many drinks are needed?_____

Children should get used to doing the sums in this way, and should do them in their head if they can. When discussing the work with your child, use the language of multiplication – 'multiply', 'times', etc. – as much as possible.

Multiplication with all tables

To learn to solve more complex multiplication sums and problems, using all the tables.

Can you solve these multiplication sums and problems?

1.   10   x   2   = ☐

2.   7   x   10   = ☐

3.   2   x   9   = ☐

4.   4   x   8   = ☐

5.   3   x   6   = ☐

6.   10   x   4   = ☐

7.   6   x   7   = ☐

8.   7   x   5   = ☐

9.   2   x   3   = ☐

10.   2   x   2   = ☐

If 9 policemen each arrest 5 burglars with 2 sacks of loot each, how many sacks of loot are there?_____

If there are 4 cakes in a packet and 5 packets in a box, how many cakes are there in 10 boxes?_____

How many boots are needed for 2 eleven-a-side tug-of-war teams?_____

If a woman is 3 times her son's age and her son is twice the age of his sister, how old is the woman if her daughter is 6?_____

Get your child to work out these problems in his or her head as much as possible.

Set your own problems, using the words 'pairs' and 'doubles'.

To learn to solve simple division sums and problems, using all the tables.

Division with all tables

Can you solve these division sums and problems?

1. 63 ÷ 9 = ☐
2. 48 ÷ 6 = ☐
3. 72 ÷ 8 = ☐
4. 28 ÷ 7 = ☐
5. 48 ÷ 8 = ☐
6. 7 ÷ 7 = ☐
7. 18 ÷ 6 = ☐
8. 90 ÷ 9 = ☐
9. 6 ÷ 6 = ☐
10. 9 ÷ 9 = ☐

A sandwich shop makes 100 sandwiches. If 19 people need lunch, how many sandwiches does each person get, and how many sandwiches are left over?_____

The sandwich shop sells 200 cans of fizzy drink in one school week. If the shop sells the same amount on every day of the same week, how many cans does it sell a day?_____

A sandwich shop uses 17 loaves a day. If it buys 10 boxes of bread and there are 15 loaves in each box, how many days will the bread last?_____   How many loaves are left over? _____

Encourage your child to use tables to solve the sums mentally. Discuss strategies with your child, such as multiplying the units first and then the tens, adding them both together.

5

Division with all tables

To learn to solve more complex division sums and problems, using all the tables.

Can you solve these division sums and problems?

1. 63 ÷ 7 =
2. 6 ÷ 6 =
3. 72 ÷ 9 =
4. 48 ÷ 6 =
5. 72 ÷ 8 =
6. 36 ÷ 6 =
7. 56 ÷ 8 =
8. 64 ÷ 8 =
9. 63 ÷ 9 =
10. 35 ÷ 7 =

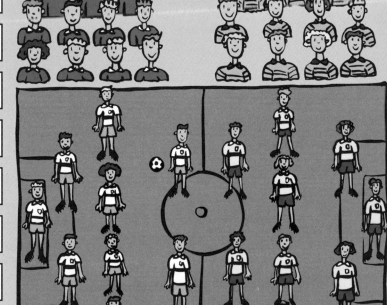

If there are 66 players, how many eleven-a-side football teams can be made?_____

How many people are left over if there are 97 people and only 17 five-seater cars to carry them?_____

If there are 39 children in a class, and they each need a rubber, how many more rubbers are needed if the school buys 2 boxes of 17 rubbers?_____

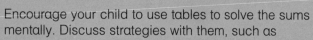

Encourage your child to use tables to solve the sums mentally. Discuss strategies with them, such as multiplying the units first and then the tens, adding them both together.

6

To learn to solve problems using
two-digit multiplication and division.

Multiplication and division

If the bags of treasure each contain 20 gold pieces, how many gold pieces are there altogether?_____

If the pirates each have an equal share, how many gold pieces does each pirate get?_____

If each treasure chest contains 10 gold necklaces, 12 gold statues and 6 jewelled cups, how many pieces of treasure are there?_____

If the pirates each have an equal share, how many pieces of treasure does each pirate get?_____

If you have 58 gold pieces, how many more do you need for each pirate to get 20?_____

If each gold piece is worth £70 and 300 gold pieces are shared equally among the pirates, how many pounds' worth of gold does each pirate get?_____

Encourage your child to write down the sum he or she is going to do and then try it out, so that your child can check the answers later.

Multiplication and division

To learn to solve more complex multiplication and division problems in more than one step.

The 'Jolly Roger' pirate ship is being chased from Treasure Island by 3 enemy ships. Another 3 enemy ships arrive to help capture the 'Jolly Roger'. If there are 50 sailors on each ship, what is the total number of sailors on all the enemy ships?

If each sailor on a ship eats 6 bowls of horrible stew each day, how many bowls of stew are needed for each ship each day?

How many bowls of stew are needed a day for 4 ships?

How many bowls of stew are needed for 4 ships for 25 days?

The sailors on the 3 new enemy ships try to get on board the 'Jolly Roger'. They all get into boats that can carry 7 people. How many boats are needed for all the sailors on the three ships?

If the pirates from the 'Jolly Roger' escape in 5 small boats, how many pirates will there be in each?

You cannot have a remainder or go into decimals in these problems. Explain to your child that one boat may only have 3 people in it!

Try making up questions of your own.

To learn to solve more complex multiplication sums and problems with missing numbers (algebra).

Division equations

Can you solve these multiplication sums and problems?

1. ☐ x 6 = 30

2. 10 x ☐ = 70

3. ☐ x 9 = 45

4. 6 x ☐ = 30

5. ☐ x 8 = 64

6. 2 x ☐ = 10

7. ☐ x 6 = 6

8. 3 x ☐ = 24

9. ☐ x 7 = 56

10. 6 x ☐ = 54

How many books are there in a packet if a teacher buys 9 packets and has a total of 270 books?

_____

If the same teacher has 36 children in her class and each child uses one book every term, how many complete terms' worth of books has she bought, and how many will she have left over?

_____

A bus makes 36 journeys and can carry a total of 40 people at a time. How many people can it carry altogether?

_____

Children should always think of these sums as the reverse of division.

Get your child to write out the sums, particularly the last one, and talk to him or her about the maths involved.

Division equations

To learn to solve more complex division sums and problems with missing numbers (algebra).

Can you solve these division sums and problems?

1. $14 \div \boxed{} = 2$

2. $\boxed{} \div 8 = 9$

3. $7 \div \boxed{} = 1$

4. $\boxed{} \div 8 = 6$

5. $36 \div \boxed{} = 6$

6. $\boxed{} \div 7 = 1$

7. $9 \div \boxed{} = 1$

8. $\boxed{} \div 8 = 8$

9. $48 \div \boxed{} = 8$

10. $\boxed{} \div 9 = 2$

A workman buys 12 boxes of sand mix. If he has 144 packets of sand mix altogether, how many packets are there in a box?

If Melanie buys 13 packs of felt-tip pens for her party and has 403 pens altogether, how many packs did she buy?

John is half the age of his mother. His sister is a third of his age. How old is his sister if his mum is 42?

Encourage your child to write out the sums in reverse, as multiplications. He or she should jot numbers down and do the sums mentally, where possible.

Times tables

 To learn to reach a target number, using multiplication and division.

Here is a number trail. What number do you get at the end?
Work out the answer to a question, then use the answer to work out
the next sum until you reach the end.

5   x 2   [ ]   x   30

TRAIL

6   ÷

3   ÷

x 11

x   66

x 10   ÷ 2

÷ 11

÷ 2

Introducing square numbers

To learn to recognise square numbers and solve problems with powers.

When we times a number by itself we call the answer a **square number**. It is a bit like finding the area of a square.

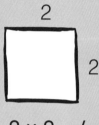

2 x 2 = 4

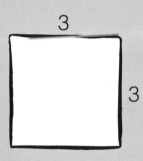

3 x 3 = 9

Look at this number. We call the little number above the large one its **power**.

2^2

In this case the power is 2, which means we multiply the number 2 times, like this.

2 x 2 = 4

What is the value of these numbers?

3^2 _____

4^2 _____

5^2 _____

6^2 _____

7^2 _____

Encourage your child to practise the notation of square numbers. Show him or her the calculation for area and explain that the 2 in cm² means 2 multiplied by 2. A calculator may help.

12

To learn to solve problems with powers greater than 2.

Powers of numbers

13

Not only do we have numbers to the power of 2. We can have numbers to any power.

Look at this example.

2^3 means $2 \times 2 \times 2 = 8$

Can you work out the value of these numbers? The first one has been done for you.

2^4	means	$2 \times 2 \times 2 \times 2$	= 16
3^3	means	_____	
4^2	means	_____	
5^3	means	_____	
2^5	means	_____	
4^3	means	_____	

 When discussing this work use words like 'squared' and 'cubed' as much as you can.

 Get your child to use a calculator to work out the biggest number possible using powers.

Estimation

 To learn to estimate answers to large multiplication sums.

Can you match the right ball to the right basket?

11 x 17

90

187

300

20 x 20

30

600

400

15 x 20

300

400

200

7 x 96

946

493

672

8 x 50

900

700

400

 With large numbers, encourage your child to round the number to the nearest 10 or multiply or divide the first digit of the number.

This will help, as it cuts down the options and gives a clear indication of the most likely answer.

To learn to estimate answers to more
complex large multiplications.

Can you match the right ball to the right basket?

With large numbers, encourage your child to round
the number to the nearest 10, or multiply or divide the
first digit of the number.

This will help, as it cuts down the options and gives
a clear indication of the most likely answer.

Multiplication of decimals

To learn to solve multiplication of decimals to one decimal place.

Can you solve these simple sums and problems?

1. 2.1
x 4

2. 3.7
x 4

3. 5.2
x 3

4. 5.9
x 4

5. 3.1
x 2

6. 3.2
x 4

7. 2.5
x 2

8. 6.3
x 2

9. 9.7
x 3

10. 4.4
x 3

11. 9.3
x 2

12. 4.2
x 3

Aisha bought 3 tickets for the concert at £2.68 each. How much money did she spend?

Each side of a square measures 3.7cm. What is the perimeter of the square?

Children should understand that if we multiply by 0.5 we are multiplying by 5 and then dividing by 10, changing the position of the decimal point.

The decimal point should be in the same place in the answer as in the sum.

To learn to solve simple sums and problems of multiplication of decimals in money.

Multiplication of decimals

Can you solve these multiplication sums and problems?

1. £
    9.15
    x   8

2. £
    1.95
    x   7

3. £
    9.59
    x   8

4. £
    6.82
    x   5

5. £
    1.80
    x   8

6. £
    1.91
    x   8

7. £
    1.89
    x   6

8. £
    7.62
    x   5

9. £
    7.25
    x   6

10. £
    5.08
    x   7

11. £
    9.46
    x   9

12. £
    7.21
    x   9

How many 56p lollies can you buy for £2?

How much did Nick spend if he bought 9 books at £2.75 each?

How much did it cost Razia to buy 8 party packs at £3.05 each?

To help your child with decimals in money, use £1 as a whole, 10p as a tenth (0.1), 1p as a hundredth (0.01), and so on.

Division and rounding

We often round a number up or down to its nearest 10 or 100, or to its nearest thousand or whole number.

Solve these division problems, using rounding.

How many packets, to the nearest 10, do you get if you divide a box of 1000 into packets with 9 in each? _____

How many people, to the nearest 10, went to 1 football match if the total number who went to 7 matches was 9964? _____

Calculate, to the nearest whole number, 7 divided by 4. _____

Fill in this chart, rounding each number to the nearest 10. The first one has been done for you.

Number	Rounding
9	10
17	_____
24	_____
109	_____
99	_____

To learn to solve simple division problems with decimals using 2, 3, 4 and 5 times tables.

Decimals

19

Can you solve these simple division problems?

1. $3\overline{)8.4}$ 2. $2\overline{)1.38}$ 3. $5\overline{)8.5}$ 4. $3\overline{)9.39}$

5. $2\overline{)9.6}$ 6. $4\overline{)6.20}$ 7. $5\overline{)7.5}$ 8. $4\overline{)3.32}$

9. $3\overline{)8.1}$ 10. $5\overline{)1.90}$ 11. $2\overline{)4.2}$ 12. $4\overline{)9.44}$

How many toys can you buy at 9p each if you have £7.20 to spend?

_____

How many 6p chewy sweets can you buy if you have £1.08?

_____

How many 7cm pieces of wood can you make out of 2.31 metres?

_____

 Division with decimals is the same as any other division, except that the decimal point should be in the same position in the answer as in the sum.

Use money to explain the difference a decimal point can make – i.e. there is a big difference between £2.50 and £250.

Decimals

To learn to solve simple division problems in decimals, using all tables.

Can you solve these decimal sums and problems?

1. $6\overline{)2.970}$ 2. $9\overline{)4.68}$ 3. $6\overline{)1.578}$ 4. $7\overline{)7.14}$

5. $8\overline{)9.120}$ 6. $9\overline{)5.85}$ 7. $7\overline{)7.875}$ 8. $6\overline{)6.72}$

9. $8\overline{)1.952}$ 10. $9\overline{)8.28}$ 11. $8\overline{)5.336}$ 12. $7\overline{)1.05}$

A bridge is 1.19km long. How many 7m lengths of metal are needed to cover the top?

_____

A tree is 9.792m high. If it is cut into 8 pieces, how long is each piece?

_____

Children often try to divide the whole number by the decimal or put the decimal point in the wrong place. Talk to your child about the need for accuracy and encourage him or her to use the correct notation in the answers.

To learn to balance simple number division problems.

Can you balance out these division sums?

Using the numbers given, fill in the missing numbers.

10 ÷ 2		15 ÷		21 ÷		35 ÷

     7

| 18 ÷ 6 | | 30 ÷ | | 42 ÷ | | 49 ÷ |

     7

| 12 ÷ 4 | | 24 ÷ 8 | | 50 ÷ 10 | | 70 ÷ |

     5

| 108 ÷ 12 | | 81 ÷ | | 2 ÷ 4 | | 1 ÷ |

     0.5

 Get your child to work out the first sum properly and then see in how many other ways he or she can get that answer through division.

Problems using information

 To learn to read information and use it to solve multiplication and division problems.

Hotel rooms (per night)
Sombre Sombrero   £23.50
Mostly Mosquitoes   £37.25
Rowdy Roger's   £26.95

Boat Hire
1 hour   £2.38
Economy ticket (5 hours)   £10

Windsurfing
1 hour   £3.96
Economy ticket (5 hours)   £12

Disco
1 night   £7.50
Economy ticket (5 nights) £30

Sun-lounger hire   (95p per hour)

Which is cheaper: 2 nights at the Sombre Sombrero, or 3 nights at Mostly Mosquitoes?

_____

How much more does it cost to stay 5 nights at Rowdy Roger's than 5 nights at the Sombre Sombrero?

_____

How many nights could you stay at each hotel for £100? You may find it easier if you round the numbers to the nearest £1 or £10.

_____

_____

_____

 With the first question, see if your child can find an easier way to work out the answer than multiplying and subtracting.

With the other questions, concentrate on your child's rounding and estimating skills.

To learn to solve more complex multiplication and division problems using a chart.

Problems using information

Look at the price list on the opposite page. Work out the difference between the hourly and economy charges for boat hire, windsurfing and the disco. Say if you think it is worth getting one of the special economy tickets or not, and why.

_____

_____

_____

Complete this chart giving prices for sun-lounger hire. After 5 hours the price goes down to 45p per hour!

No. of hours	1	2	3	4	5	6
Price	95p					

A boat trip costs £1 per person. A group of 5 people can go for £6. Is this a bargain?

_____

Explain your answer.

_____

_____

It is sometimes difficult for children to use maths instead of instinctive answers, such as 'I wouldn't go windsurfing for five hours.'

Explain to your child the importance of being able to work out mathematical answers to problems.

Long multiplication

To learn to solve simple long multiplication sums and problems.

Use long multiplication to solve these problems.

1. 76
    x 44

    _____

2. 42
    x 24

    _____

3. 16
    x 68

    _____

4. 92
    x 15

    _____

5. 57
    x 93

    _____

6. 57
    x 38

    _____

7. 78
    x 57

    _____

8. 78
    x 55

    _____

If there are 26 children in a class and 39 classes go to the pantomime, how many children are there altogether?

_____

_____

If a woman spends 45 hours a week at work, how many hours does she work all year if she never has a holiday?

_____

It may help to break down each sum into stages, writing these down next to the sum. For example, 36 x 48 means (6 units x 48) + (3 tens x 48).

To learn to solve more complex long multiplication sums and problems.

Long multiplication

Solve these long multiplication sums and problems.

1. 333
    x 87

2. 474
    x 35

3. 275
    x 13

4. 318
    x 15

5. 886
    x 41

6. 399
    x 41

7. 692
    x 76

8. 899
    x 69

If a hotel is full every week for 36 weeks and it can take 392 people when it is full, how many people stayed there during this time?

An aeroplane company has 12 aeroplanes. Each one can carry 127 people. How many people can it carry if it uses all its planes?

3-digit addition is quite a leap from 2-digit addition, because of the multiplication of hundreds. Get your child to break down the sums and problems into stages and set them out on another piece of paper so that he or she does not confuse the numbers being carried with those being added.

Solving problems

To learn to solve problems by comparing answers.

Solve these problems.

Who has more cars, if John has 9 boxes of 12 cars and Terry has 103 cars? _____

A farmer has 17 rows of carrots in a field, with 25 carrots in each row. How many carrots has he altogether?_____

Two milkmen are trying to supply Greentown with milk. Fred's Fantasy Float has 14 crates with 11 bottles in each crate. John Jolly's float has 7 crates with 21 bottles in each crate. Who can deliver the most milk?_____

If a supermarket buys 29 boxes of eggs and there are a dozen eggs in a box, how many eggs does the supermarket have?

_____

Sarah's school has 9 classes in it, and each class has 29 pupils. Susan's school has 18 classes and 14 children in each class. Which school has the most children?_____

A block of flats has 29 flats on each floor. If it has 12 floors, how many flats does it have?_____

Encourage your child to use the language and skills of estimation and calculation here. First isolate the numbers required to do the sum, regardless of the context, and then use these to set out the correct sum.

To learn to solve more complex problems by using numbers from previous questions.

Solving problems

Solve these problems.

8 children and their bags fit into a minibus. How many minibuses are needed to take 72 children on a camping holiday? _____

The children arrive at the camp site and another 4 schools are already there, with just as many children from each school. How many children are there in the camp altogether? _____

A tent holds five children. How many tents are needed for all the children in the camp? _____

To go on a trip, the schools hire some coaches. Each coach can carry 40 children. How many coaches are needed to carry everyone? _____

One coach gets lost and ends up on a mountain. How many children turn up at the right place? _____

The helicopter rescued 8 people at a time from the lost coach. How many trips did it have to make to rescue the children and the driver before everyone was safe? _____

 Encourage your child to make an estimate before continuing with his or her calculations and ask if the answer seems correct. If your child ends up with huge remainders, ask 'Is it sensible?' Get your child to check his or her answers.

Solving Problems

 To learn to spot complex number patterns with multiplication and division problems.

Can you solve these number patterns?
Watch out, some of them are quite difficult to spot!

1.
[4] [ ] [12] [ ] [ ] [24]

2.
[3] [ ] [ ] [12] [ ] [ ] [21]

3.
[3] [6] [12] [ ] [ ] [96]

4.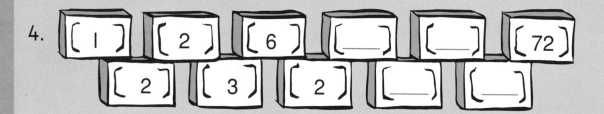
[1] [2] [6] [ ] [ ] [72]
[2] [3] [2] [ ] [ ]

5.
[10] [5] [20] [ ] [40]
[2] [4] [ ] [4]

6.
[5] [40] [4] [ ] [ ] [60] [5]
[8] [10] [12] [8] [ ] [ ]

Children will need support with patterns 4, 5 and 6. The maths is not complex but the pattern is. Take it in turn with your child to make your own patterns.

Have a competition to see who can come up with the most complex number patterns.

To learn to use answers from other questions to check calculations.

Multiplication and division

Can you finish this number puzzle?

Across

1   60 multiplied by 2
4   9 x 3
6   Half of 150
8   26 times 4
10 The product of 9 and 5
12 3 x 3
14 The product of 8 and 5
15 300 ÷ 10

Down

2   3 times 9
3   Half of 1
4   20 times 10
5   14 shared by 2
7   28 divided by 2
9   7^2
11 50 multiplied by 10
13 3 x 11

Get your child to check the answers by making sure the numbers reading downwards agree with those reading across.

Multiplication and division

To learn to solve problems with decimal and multiplication and division questions.

Scores	
Great Britain	23.8m
Usa	22.9m
France	21.6m

The javelin results are worked out by finding the average distance thrown by each country in the competition.

If each country has four throws, what is the total distance thrown by each country?

Great Britain _____

USA _____

France _____

Kenya threw 27.4m on its first throw, 24.8m on its second throw and 21.1 m on its third throw. If its average throw was 20m, what was its final terrible throw?_____

_____

_____

In the 400m relay race, four athletes each run 100m. Look at the total times for each country and work out how long each 100m took, on average, for each country.

Australia _____

Great Britain _____

Egypt _____

SCORES	
Australia	38.92 seconds
Great Britain	37.04 seconds
Egypt	34.18 seconds

Make sure your child grasps the concept of averages and can describe the kind of work needed to solve each problem.

To learn to solve problems with decimals and read decimal charts.

Multiplication and division

SCORES	
France	5.4/5.5/5.5/5.9
Germany	4.9/4.6/4.6/5.0
Great Britain	5.9/6.0/5.7/5.8
New Zealand	6.3/6.4/5.9/5.8
USA	6.1/5.9/6.2/6.3

The score for each country is worked out by four scores being added together and then averaged out by dividing by the number of scores (4). What was the final score for each country when rounded off to 2 decimal places?

France

Germany

Great Britain

New Zealand

USA

Which country won the competition?

The total scores for the other countries are given below. What was the average score for each one?

Argentina	Austria	Egypt	Italy	Sweden
3.45	24.12	21.32	10.04	16.96

Make sure children know that to work out the average for each operation they must divide by 4. Get them to explain each step of their work.

31

Answers page

page 2

x	3	5	1	7	9
9	27	45	9	63	81
7	21	35	7	49	63
5	15	25	5	35	45
3	9	15	3	21	27
1	3	5	1	7	9

x	2	6	4	8	10
10	20	60	40	80	100
2	4	12	8	16	20
4	8	24	16	32	40
6	12	36	24	48	60
8	16	40	32	64	80

x	1	2	5	3	7
3	3	6	15	9	21
4	4	8	20	12	28
8	8	16	40	24	56
10	10	20	50	30	70
6	6	12	30	18	42

x	2	3	4	5	6
7	14	21	28	35	42
8	16	24	32	40	48
9	18	27	36	45	54
10	20	30	40	50	60
2	4	6	8	10	12

odd, even, even, 0 or 5,0

page 3
1.10, 2.28, 3.15, 4.60, 5.32, 6.24, 7.54,
8.14, 9.8, 10.48; 96, 64, 55

page 4
1.20, 2.70, 3.18, 4.32, 5.18, 6.40,
7.42, 8.35, 9.6, 10.4; 90, 200, 44, 36

page 5
1.7, 2.8, 3.9, 4.4, 5.6, 6.1, 7.3, 8.10, 9.1,
10.1; 5 r 5, 40, 8, 14

page 6
1.9, 2.1, 3.8, 4.8, 5.9, 6.6, 7.7, 8.8, 9.7,
10.5; 6, 12, 5

page 7
180, 36, 140, 28, 42, £4200

page 8
300, 300, 1200, 30 000, 22, 10

page 9
1.5, 2.7, 3.5, 4.5, 5.8, 6.5, 7.1, 8.8,
9.8, 10.9; 30, 7 r 18, 1440

page 10
1.7, 2.72, 3.7, 4.48, 5.6, 6.7, 7.9,
8.64, 9.6, 10.18
12, 31, 7

page 11
10, 3, 5, 2, 33, 2, 33, 330, 15

page 12
9, 16, 25, 36, 49

page 13
27, 16, 125, 32, 64

page 14
187, 400, 300, 672, 400

page 15
100, 144, 153, 252, 172

page 16
1.8.4, 2.14.8, 3.15.6, 4.23.6, 5.6.2,
6.12.8, 7.5, 8.12.6, 9.29.1, 10.13.2, 11.18.6,
12.12.6; £8.04, 14.8cm

page 17
1.£73.20 2.£13.65 3.£76.72 4.£34.10
5.£14.40 6.£15.28 7.£11.34 8.£38.10
9.£43.50 10.£35.56 11.£85.14 12.£64.89
3, £24.75, £24.40

page 18
110, 1420 2; 20, 20, 110, 100

page 19
1.2.8 2.0.69 3.1.7 4.3.13 5.4.8 6.1.55
7.1.5 8.0.83 9.2.7 10.0.38 11.2.1 12.2.36
80, 18, 33

page 20
1.0.495 2.0.52 3.0.263 4.1.02 5.1.14
6.0.65 7.1.125 8.1.12 9.0.244 10.0.92
11.0.667 12.0.15; 170, 1.224m

page 21
5 & 3, 3 & 5, 3 & 10, 6 & 7, 3, 14, 9 & 9, 2

page 22
2 nights at the Sombre Sombrero, £17.25,
Sombre Sombrero 4, Mostly Mosquitoes 2,
Rowdy Roger's 3

page 23
Boat hire – yes; you save £1.90;
Windsurfing – yes; you save £7.80;
Disco – yes; you save £7.50
£1.90, £2.85, £3.80, £4.75, £5.20
No, because if each person bought their
own ticket, a group of five people could
go for £5;

page 24
1.3344, 2.1008, 3.1088, 4.1380, 5.5301,
6.2166, 7.4446, 8.4290; 1014, 2340

page 25
1.28971, 2.16590, 3.3575, 4.4770,
5.36326, 6.16359, 7.52592, 8.62031
14112, 1524

page 26
John, 425, Fred's Fantasy Float, 348,
Sarah's school, 348

page 27
9, 360, 72, 9, 320, 6

page 28
1. 4, 8, 12, 16, 20 24
2. 3, 6, 9, 12, 15, 18, 21
3. 3, 6, 12, 24, 48, 96
4. 1, 2, 6, 12, 36, 72
   2 3 2 3 2
5. 10, 5, 20, 10, 40
   2 4 2 4
6. 5, 40, 4, 48, 6, 60, 5
   8 10 12 8 10 12

page 29

1	2	0		2	7
	7	5		0	
1			1	0	4
4	5				9
	0		3		
4	0		3	0	

page 30
GB 95.2m, USA 91.6m, France 86.4m
6.7m
Australia 9.73 seconds,
Great Britain 9.26 seconds,
Egypt 8.54 seconds

page 31
5.58, 4.78, 5.85, 6.1, 6.13;
USA, 0.86, 6.03, 5.33, 2.51, 4.24